A GUIDE TO SOCIA MARKETIN

THE EASYWAY

MARKET AND ENHANCE YOUR BUSINESS
THROUGH SOCIAL MEDIA

MICHAEL LANE

Editor: Roger Sproston

Easyway Guides

Easyway Guides

British Library Cataloguing in Publication data. A Catalogue record of this book is available from the British Library.

ISBN

978-1-913342-76-0

Cover Design by BW Studio
Derby
Printed by 4 Edge www.4edge.co.uk

Whilst every effort has been made to ensure that the information contained within this book is correct at the time of going to press, the author and publisher cannot accept responsibility for any errors or omissions contained in this book.

Contents

****

INTRODUCTION TO SOCIAL MEDIA MARKETING

A typical and very general definition of social media is:

Forms of electronic communication (such as websites for social networking and microblogging) through which users create online communities to share information, ideas, personal messages, and other content (such as videos).

This more or less sums up the nature of social media. Forms of electronic communication.

Social media, particularly in the 21st Century has taken off massively and is rapidly becoming the dominant forum for all those people and businesses who wish to promote their products. This book, aptly entitled A Guide to Social Media Marketing, The Easyway, sets out to show how a business can set up social media sites and target those sites so that they achieve the most effective coverage and promotion.

The main thing is to understand the exact nature of social media, what it is and how best to utilise it. There are some grandiose claims about how social media has reduced the need to go out and find customers as customers are now all connected. To a limited extent that is true, but social media platforms should be seen as an adjunct to all other forms of marketing. The main point is that to reach customers you need to know how to set up and utilise pages on the various social media sites.

Traditionally, those wishing to promote a product would use (still do very much use) the more established methods, such as newspaper, television and radio. However, if you have deep pockets you are OK but, in the case of existing small businesses money is tight and your marketing cannot stretch to this. What you can do is to effectively utilise social media platforms, which are largely free. That is the beauty of social media! Whilst it is still difficult to compete with big business at least you can be in there with a fighting chance if you do it yourself.

The advantage of small businesses and start ups is that they can, in the world of social media, respond more quickly than larger businesses, as larger businesses, encumbered that they are with layers of bureaucracy, can be slow to change thereby losing the competitive edge.

Social media influencers

Social media influencers are users with large followings on major social networks, primarily YouTube, Instagram, Snapchat, Facebook, Twitter, individual blogs or, most likely, some combination of these. Social media has created new opportunities for marketers to expand their strategy beyond traditional mass-media channels. Many use influencers to increase the reach of their marketing messages. Online influencers who curate personal brands have become marketing assets because of their relationship with their followers.

A word of caution. As has been pointed out, and is worth repeating, don't be blinded by people waxing lyrical about how social media is going to take over the world. The reality is that it sits alongside other forms of marketing. The world is full of social media marketers who, for a (usually large) fee, will set up pages for you and formulate a campaign. However, given that social media is awash with people promoting products, quite a lot of those ineffectively targeted, you have to be very careful. Basically, you could end up throwing a lot of time and money away and achieve very little, as people have been doing for years with the more traditional forms of marketing. With time and effort, you can set up your own campaign, at minimal cost.

What you need to clearly understand at the outset is:

- *the nature of your product*
- *how to target the product*
- *who the end users are,*

and then find your audience (know who will buy it) and, of course, make sure you have a functioning business.

You then need to understand the nature of the major platforms in the world of social media and how they operate and how you can set up your own accounts with them and then begin to utilise them effectively. In this book, we will concentrate on setting up the following 6 platforms:

- Facebook
- YouTube
- LINKEDIN
- Twitter

- Instagram
- Pinterest

There are others, with more developing all the time, but I will be concentrating on the more established ones. You will find that this is enough to be getting on with, as setting up these accounts and using them effectively for business takes time and effort. It is highly advisable to set up one main site first to get into the swing of things and raise your awareness. If and when you feel ready you can progress through the sites.

This practical guide should enable you to assemble an arsenal of marketing tools, through social media, that you can develop as you go. It must be emphasised that the book is very much a 'how to' manual as, not only does it describe the merits of each platform, it also provides a step-by-step guide to setting up accounts with each site and the technical side of how to build up a marketing campaign. I have attempted to make it as clear and simple as possible, although it should be realised that at times the processes can appear very detailed.

Stay with it, concentrate on one platform to begin with and you will reap the rewards.

I will start with the big one, Facebook, which is one of the most commonly used sites for social media marketing.

****

Chapter 1

FACEBOOK

Facebook as A Social Media Marketing Tool

> **Introduction to Facebook**
>
> *For the uninitiated, Facebook is a social networking website where users can post comments, share photographs, and post links to news or other interesting content on the web, chat live, and watch short-form video. Shared content can be made publicly accessible, or it can be shared only among a select group of friends or family, or with a single person.* ***It is a very valuable tool for business.***

How Facebook Began

Facebook began in February of 2004 as a social network at Harvard University. It was created by Mark Zuckerberg along with Edward Saverin, plus several others, all students at the college. It wasn't until 2006 that Facebook opened up to anyone 13 years or older and took off, rapidly overtaking MySpace as the most popular social network in the world. Facebook's success can be attributed to its ability to appeal to both people and businesses and its ability to interact with sites around the web by providing a single login that works across multiple sites.

Facebook is user-friendly and open to everyone. Even the least technically-minded people can sign up and begin posting on Facebook. Although it started out as a way to keep in touch or reconnect with long-lost friends, it rapidly became the darling of businesses that were able to closely target an audience and deliver ads directly to the people most likely to want their products or services.

Facebook makes it simple to share photos, text messages, videos, status posts and feelings. The site is entertaining and a regular daily stop for many users.

Unlike some social network sites, Facebook does not allow adult content. When users transgress and are reported, they are banned from the site. Facebook also provides a customizable set of privacy controls, so users can protect their information from getting to third-party individuals.

The Key Features of Facebook

Facebook supports group pages, fan pages, and business pages that let businesses use the site as a vehicle for social media marketing.

*

Introduction to Facebook pages

At the outset it is important to realise that a Facebook Business Page is a free opportunity for businesses to increase brand awareness and generate sales. As we have seen, conventional marketing can be very expensive and often, if not targeted properly, doesn't really produce anything of value. Social media, on the other hand, though costly in terms of time, can be of immense help if handled properly.

All of the interactions within Facebook are based on two elements: **Profiles and pages**. A *profile* is based around the person and introduces that person. It is created for an individual looking to present, or promote, his or herself. A *page* introduces a company or business. An individual can create a profile and a business page.

A profile can add friends (essentially other people who use Facebook). These friends can be all sorts of people, family, real time friends and acquaintances. The page, on the other hand, can have likes and followers. Likes refer to the number of people who like the page and also the company in question. The likes can be any number of people who cannot be readily identified.

First things first-creating a Business page

There are a number of steps in the creation of Facebook pages. The first thing is that it is easier to have a personal account to be able to create a business account. Alternatively, you can enter Facebook.com/pages and create a page. Follow these simple steps below to create your Facebook business page:

1. *Register for a Facebook Business Page*-As mentioned, Facebook business pages are usually created using a personal Facebook account, so you'll need to first log in to your Facebook account. In the right-hand side of the blue toolbar, find and click the "Create" button.

2. *Select "Page" from the Menu*-A drop-down list will appear after clicking "Create." Select the first option, "Page," to create your Facebook Business Page.

3. *Enter the name of the page*-Once you have created a page you should enter the name of the page. For example, if you are a publishing company it can be called XYZ publishing.

When you have named the page, you can click on the type of business you are operating. There are six options to choose from:

- Local business place
- Company, organisation or institution
- Brand or product
- Artists, band or public figure
- Entertainment (promotion)
- Cause or community

Only when you have chosen the appropriate option can you move on to the next step. This is where you fill in the 'About' info details before adding your website details. Once all of this has been completed Facebook will assign you a unique URL for your page.

It's now time to get down to the specifics of developing your page!

Options to choose

Choose the *preferred page audience*. For example, if your page has content for specific age groups, say over 18's, then this must be made clear to the audience. There are a number of page settings that you can choose which will greatly assist the functioning of your site.

In the Settings panel, you can configure almost every element of your Facebook account, including basic items such as your name, how you receive notifications, and who can interact with you and view your content.

There are settings to regulate the visibility of your page-you can choose who can view your page; you can choose who can post on your page to avoid millions of unwanted and unnecessary posts; you can choose to target the posts to an appropriate audience and also block spam.

There are many other settings which enable you to really tailor the page. For details of these go to: www.facebook.com/help. Once you have filled in all of the details required in the settings, you can then continue with the next stage of development.

Posting profile pictures

To add a Facebook profile picture or change your current profile picture:

1. Click your profile picture in the top right of Facebook.
2. Click in the bottom right of your profile picture.
3. Choose a photo or add a frame.
4. Click to crop your photo and then click **Save**.

For best quality, your profile picture should be at least *320 pixels wide and 320 pixels tall.* (You will see many versions of what is required, best follow Facebook guidelines)

Updating your picture

When updating your profile picture, you can:

- Upload a photo from your computer or phone.
- Add a frame to an existing or new picture.
- Select a photo you've already uploaded or one you're tagged in.

Cover photos

A cover photo is the larger photo at the top of your profile, above your profile picture. Like your profile picture, cover photos are public, which means anyone visiting your profile will be able to see them.

To add or change your cover photo:

1. Click your profile picture in the top right of Facebook.

2. Click **Edit Cover Photo**. If you don't currently have a cover photo, click **Add Cover Photo**.

3. Click **Upload Photo** to upload a new photo from your computer or **Select Photo** to pick a photo from one of your Facebook albums. Once you choose a photo, you can reposition it by clicking the image and dragging it up or down.

4. Click **Save Changes**.

Note: Your cover image has to be at least 720 pixels wide.

Adding a Call-to-Action button on your Facebook page

A call to action on Facebook is a button that appears on your business page and aims to get your target audience to take action with your business. These people may be those who follow your page, those that have liked the page or other target audience that may find you on Facebook in various ways. It is very important for you to guide your audience and tell them what to do on your page. Many people assume that people by themselves will understand what they should do on a page; however, it pays to give them clear instructions so they can engage with your business.

Remember, communication is the essence of all successful marketing campaigns.

To add a call-to-action button to your Page, you'll need to be an admin, editor, moderator or advertiser (which you will be).

To add a call-to-action button to your Page:

1. From your News Feed, click **Pages** in the left menu.
2. Go to your Page.
3. Click **+ Add a Button** below your Page's cover photo.
4. Select a button from the dropdown menu and follow the on-screen instructions.
5. Click **Save**.

Once the button has been created, you can test your button:

1. Click your button.
2. Select **Test Button**.
3. It's that simple!

Posting on your Facebook business page

Once you have created your Facebook business page, and you are ready to create content, then there are some simple steps to follow.

The Technicalities of posting content

You can post content onto your pages either from your mobile or from your computer.

Posting from your desktop

Open Facebook. Go to https://www.facebook.com/. This will open your Facebook News Feed if you're logged in. If you aren't logged in, enter your email address (or phone number) and password in the top-right side of the page.

Go to the page where you want to post. Depending on where you want to create your post, this will vary:

- **Your page** - You can create a post for your page from the top of the News Feed.

- **A friend's page** - Click the search bar at the top of the screen, type in a friend's name, click their name, then click their profile image.

- **A group** - Click **Groups** on the left side of the page, click the **Groups** tab, and then click the group you want to go to.

Click the post box. This box is at the top of the News Feed. If you're posting to a friend's page or a group page, you'll find the post box below the cover photo.

Add text to your post. Type your content into the post box. You can also add a coloured background by clicking one of the color blocks below the text box. Coloured backgrounds are only supported for posts of 130 characters or fewer.

Add more content to your post. If you want to add more to your post, click one of the options located below the post box:

- **Photo/Video** - Allows you to select a photo or video from your computer to upload to the post.

- **Tag Friends** - Allows you to select a friend or group of friends to tag in the post. Tagged friends will receive the post on their own pages.
- **Check in** - Lets you add an address or a location to your post.
- **Feeling/Activity** - Lets you select an emotion or activity to add to the post.

Click POST. (the blue button in the bottom-right corner of the window).

Posting from a mobile

Open Facebook. The Facebook app icon looks like a white "f" on a dark-blue background. Facebook will open to your News Feed if you're already logged in.

If you aren't already logged in, enter your email address (or phone number) and password, then tap **Log in.**

Go to the page where you want to post. Depending on where you want to create your post, this will vary:

- **Your page** - You can create a post for your page from the top of the News Feed.
- **A friend's page** - Tap the search bar at the top of the screen, type in a friend's name, tap their name, then tap their profile image.
- **A group** - Tap **Groups**, tap the **Groups** tab, and tap your group.

Tap the post box. This box is at the top of the News Feed. If you're posting to a friend's page, it's below the photo section that's near the top of their page. If you're posting to a group, you'll find the box just below the cover photo.

There will generally be a phrase like "Write something" or "What's on your mind?" in the box.

Upload a photo or a video. Tap **Photo/Video** near the middle of the post screen, then select a photo or video to upload and tap **Done**. Doing so adds the photo or video to your post. You can tap multiple photos or videos to upload them all at once. Skip this step if you want to upload a text-only post.

Add text to your post. Tap the text field, then type in the text for your post. You can also tap a coloured circle along the middle of the screen to set a background for your post. You can only add colour to posts with 130 characters or fewer.

Tap Add To Your Post- It's in the middle of the screen. This will bring up the following post options:

- **Photo/Video** - Add more photos or videos.
- **Check In** - Allows you to add an address or location to your post.
- **Feeling/Activity/Sticker** - Lets you add an emotion, activity, or emoji.
- **Tag People** - Allows you to add a person to this post. Doing so puts the post on their page as well.

Select a post option to add more to the post. This is completely optional. If you don't want to add more to the post, skip to the next step.

Tap POST. It's in the top-right corner of the screen. Doing so will create your post and add it to the page you're on.

Remember, Your home page is what you see when you log into Facebook. It includes your News Feed, the constantly updating list of posts from your friends, groups you're in, Pages you follow and more. It is very important to get this right. Below are a few tips on posting onto your page.

Technical specifications

There is a lot of varying advice concerning the specifications for a Facebook post. Basically, as a rule of thumb, newsfeed images should be 472 x 472 pixels and have an actual ratio of 236 x 197 pixels and the image should be 504 x 504 pixels. Confused! Don't worry there are several useful sites, including Facebook itself which can offer advice and guidance. Two such sites are picmonkey.com and canva.com.

Posting content to a page-Bring Your Page Alive!

It's very important to emphasize that you need to bring personality to a page, you need to bring it alive in order to convince people to buy your product. For example, if you are selling clothes, you can't just put a picture of what it is you are selling and expect people to buy it! You need to build up a profile of what you are selling, perhaps post a video, and give the page a personality.

The main point is that, on social media sites in particular, you need to connect to people emotionally. If a company is able to advertise a product on television they can easily do this. However, a business page on Facebook, and all the other platforms mentioned in this book, will need more work.

You are connecting with a lot of other users, your posts have the ability to go viral and you need to engage people so they will want to explore more. That means connecting to your audience emotionally. This is a principle that underpins all forms of marketing. If you can't connect with people and their emotions then you are fighting a losing battle.

Key points when setting up and running a Facebook page

When creating your business page it is very important to have a real sense of who you are and what your company stands for. In short, you need to know and understand your own identity and business identity. Make sure that you have a real feel for it. This will then feed through to your business page. It will start to connect emotionally with users. Your Facebook page will be a shop window for your business and what you sell there. It is important to keep in mind your main business motives and goals.

Consistency in your presentation and postings

Make sure that your postings to your business page are timed consistently so people are not confused. This might seem obvious but it is easy to slip up and become sloppy. Look at another successful company's schedule and arrive at your own schedule that suits your company. Make sure that you know when people are most active on Facebook, usually the early evening and time your postings in accordance with this.

In addition, make sure that your updates are as frequent as possible so that your pages remain updated. As stated, you should post in the evening as this is when most people expect new posts. As your company grows, you will need to increase the frequency of your posts. Keep the information coherent and don't overload people as they will turn away from your pages and go elsewhere. Managing a Facebook page can be time consuming but it is very important to get it right at the outset as you are creating social media pages as an important tool to market your business and enhance your profile.

Strategies for Facebook Pages

Useful websites to look at when planning your Facebook strategy:

www.postplanner.com/advanced-facebook-marketing-strategies-for-pros

blog.hootsuite.com/facebook-marketing-tips

neilpatel.com/blog/new-facebook-fan-pages

www.thebalancesmb.com/effective-facebook-marketing-strategies

www.socialmediaexaminer.com/five-facebook-only-strategies-for...

roelmanarang.com/effective-facebook-marketing-strategy

Facebook groups

Facebook groups are absolutely vital for marketing your product. This is because they allow you to interact with a highly targeted audience .Generally, people will join groups only if they have a specific need, and they look to people within that group to fulfil that need. The beauty of groups is that you can increase your awareness of what customers want and also advertise your business to them. Currently, you can join up to 6,000 groups. There are more, but 6,000 is the limit (check this detail as it can be subject to change).

Joining a group

If you want to join a group, click on the Groups tab on your Facebook profile and you will be redirected to the discover groups page. You can then search for different groups based on keywords, or find groups based on the pages that you have liked or the interests that Facebook is aware that you have.

For a business, the ideal thing is to type the name of the kind of business that you do. If you publish books for example, then just type books and you will come across multiple groups who are involved in that area.

Some groups are public and some are private. If it is a closed group then you will have to send a join request that will then have to be approved by the admin. You can click on a description of a group to find out more about the interests of that group and the rules of engagement.

Creating your own Group-Creating a community around what you sell

If you are in business, the best thing that you can do is to create a community around your product. In this way you will be able to directly engage with your customers. Unlike pages, groups are far more engaging and you will have active customers who will be interested in what you are selling.

You can create a group by clicking on the groups tab on the left hand side of your profile. You will have to name your group-make sure that the name is a catchy one that people will relate to and remember. Then you should add a few friends to start with to create the group. You should add a cover photo which will entice the audience.

Expanding your group

If you want to get more people in your group, there are several things that you can do. You can promote your group on your website and also your Facebook page. You can also get access to email subscription groups and then email a group invite to personal customers. You can also search for groups on Facebook and join them, if allowed.

How are you doing? Facebook Analytics

As we have seen, Facebook is a platform with a diverse number of users, with each user having a different way of interacting with your page and also your brand. Facebook Analytics helps you to market your product by giving you detailed information about potential customers who follow your page. Using this information, you can create targeted posts and learn about the kind of interaction that is popular with your audience. To start the process, go to your business page and click on **insight.** The three sections that you see now will tell you important things about your page:

- The number of people who liked your page in the last week
- The number of people who saw your posts
- The number of people who engaged with your posts.

Engaging means liking, sharing or commenting on what you have posted. The page likes are important for your business because they not only tell you about how many followers you are gaining but also explains where the likes are coming from. You will be able to tell whether people like your page because of your posts or for any other reason, such as a Facebook ad.

You can specifically find out the contribution of your ad campaign on the number of likes that you have got by clicking or dragging on a specific item.

The next section is the *post reach section*, which is the most important. This shows you how many people saw your post

31

and how many people subsequently interacted with it by liking, commenting or sharing. This way you can drill down and find out what kind of posts create more engagement with your audience. You can then isolate the reasons for it to continue making posts in this vein.

****

Chapter 2

Paying For Advertising on Facebook

Facebook Ads

Having set up your Facebook Business Page, putting a lot of time, effort and thought into it, we should now consider how and when to utilise Facebook ads to enhance your Social Media marketing campaign. Understanding how to maximise the reach of Facebook Ads has become a vital part of every social media marketing strategy. Paid advertising on Facebook seems to be one of the most immediate ways to impact the reach of your content.

However, before starting an ad campaign in you will need to know certain important things.

- How well does Facebook advertising work?
- What kind of overall engagement do you get?
- What can you expect for your money, what kind of return will you get?

Thinking things through-setting up a Facebook ads campaign

You need to understand that a lot of money can be thrown towards Facebook advertisements and you can get little or no return on your investment. Facebook is awash with business pages and, just like your Facebook business page, your ad campaign needs to be well thought out and accurately targeted in order to reach the people who are your audience.

There are, like all things in business, grandiose claims about the reach of Facebook, and the reach of Facebook ads. However, stop and think. Certainly, there are billions of Facebook users but how many are interested in your business pages? How do you accurately target your ads to reach the maximum number of customers? Learning to do so is the art of building a successful ads campaign.

Set goals for your Facebook Ads

Before you attempt to create any adverts, it's very important to first think about why you're advertising and what you're aiming to achieve. By setting yourself goals ahead of going live with ads, you will have something to measure your success against. For example, if you're looking to increase downloads of your mobile app through Facebook Ads, you could set a goal of 75 downloads in the first month. This will also help you when it comes to choosing the correct objective for your Facebook ads campaign Some more example goals could be:

- Increase traffic to your website from Facebook
- Increase attendance at events

- Generate new leads
- Increase the reach of your content on Facebook
- Boost engagement for your Facebook Page

Creating the ads.

Create an account with Facebook Ads Manager.

Facebook's Ad Manager is a sophisticated dashboard that provides users with an overview of all their campaigns. The dashboard highlights an estimate of how much you're spending each day. The dashboard is organized by columns, which makes it easy to filter through your ads so you can create a custom view of your results. Key numbers like reach, frequency, and cost are readily available, making reporting on performance simple.

In order to use the Facebook Ads Manager, you'll need a Facebook Business Page (which no doubt you will have by now). This is because you can't run ads through personal profiles. Then, follow the steps below:

1. Navigate to https://www.facebook.com/business/tools/ads-manager.
2. Click the button that says "Go to Ads Manager."
3. Confirm your information on the ad account setup page.
4. Set up your payment method.
5. Save changes.

Once set up, the Ads Manager becomes the control centre for your Facebook ads.

Creating an ad

Once you log into the Ads Manager, you'll see a performance dashboard where all of your campaigns, ad sets, and ads will be listed including the results they've driven for your Facebook page. Unless you've already created an ad for your Facebook page, this dashboard will be empty.

To create a new campaign ad set, or ad through the Facebook Ad Manager, tab over to the type of ad you want to create and click the green "Create" button to the far left of these ad type

Once you're into the Ads manager, you can navigate with the menu on the left-hand side of the page. To get started with your first ad, click the green button in the top-right corner of the page.

Facebook's Ads Manager, like many social media advertising networks, is designed with your campaign objective in mind. Before getting started, Ads Manager will prompt you to choose an objective for your campaign. There are 11 different objectives to choose from. The list includes everything from general brand awareness, to getting installs of your app, to increasing traffic to your online store (see chapter 3 for more about stores). By choosing one of these objectives, you're giving Facebook a better idea of what you'd like to do so they can present you with the best-suited ad options, as below:

- Brand awareness
- Reach

- Website traffic
- Engagement
- App installs
- Video views
- Lead generation
- Messages
- Conversions
- Catalogue sales
- Store traffic

For example, if you're looking to drive more traffic to your website, then when you select this option, Facebook will prompt you to enter the URL you're looking to promote. If you're using marketing automation software, be sure to create a unique tracking URL with UTM parameters for this to ensure that you'll be able to keep track of traffic and conversions from this ad. Once selected, Facebook will then display the ad option that makes the most sense in terms of achieving this objective.

With Facebook, you have many different ways of approaching an ad campaign. They can typically fall within several categories of benefits:

- Awareness
- Objectives that generate interest in your product or service
- Boost your posts
- Promote your page

- Reach people near your business
- Increase Brand Awareness
- Increase your reach

Choose your audience.

Your next step is to configure your target audience -- you can do this for each ad set that belongs to the same campaign. If you're just starting out with paid advertising on Facebook, it's likely that you'll have to experiment with several different targeting options until you reach an audience that fits just right.

To help you narrow your focus, Facebook's targeting criteria are accompanied by an audience definition gauge. This tool - located to the right of the audience targeting fields - takes all of your selected properties into consideration in order to come up with a potential reach number.

If you're wavering between choosing a specific audience over a broad one, consider your objective. If you're looking to drive traffic, you'll probably want to focus on the type of people you know will be interested in your offering. However, if you're looking to build brand awareness or promote a widely appealing offer, you should focus on a more general audience. Facebook's built-in targeting is vast, including options such as:

- Location
- Age
- Gender
- Languages

- Relationship
- Education
- Work
- Financial
- Home
- Ethnic Affinity
- Generation
- Parents
- Politics (U.S. only)
- Life Events
- Interests
- Behaviors
- Connections

You also have the option to select a Custom Audience -- this allows you to target people on Facebook who are in your company's contact database, visited a page on your website that has a tracking pixel, or use your app or game. Once you find a group that responds well to your ads, Facebook allows you to save these audiences to be used again later -- so you may not need to dive into this step once you've been running Facebook ads for a while.

How much do you want to spend-Set your budget.
Facebook allows you to set either a daily budget or a lifetime budget. Here's how they differ from each other:

Daily budget. If you want your ad set to run continuously throughout the day, this is the option you'll want to go for. Using a daily budget means that Facebook will pace your spending per day. *Lifetime budget.* If you're looking to run your ad for a specified length of time, select lifetime budget. This means Facebook will pace your spend over the time period you set for the ad to run. To further specify your budgeting, turn to the advanced options. This option allows you to specify various things, as below.

Schedule

Choose whether or not you want your campaign to run immediately and continuously or if you want to customize the start and end dates. You can also set parameters so that your ads only run during specific hours and days of the week.

Optimization & Pricing

Choose whether or not you want to bid for your objective, clicks, or impressions. (This will alter how your ad is displayed and paid for). By doing so, you'll pay for your ad to be shown to people within your target audience that are more likely to complete your desired action, but Facebook will control what your maximum bid is.

If you don't want Facebook to set optimal bids for you, you'll want to opt for manual bidding. This option awards you full control over how much you're willing to pay per action completed. However, Facebook will provide a suggested bid based on other advertisers' behaviour to give you a sense of what you should aim for.

Delivery

Delivery type falls under two categories: standard and accelerated. Standard delivery will show your ads throughout the day, while accelerated delivery helps you reach an audience quickly for time-sensitive ads (Note: this option requires manual bid pricing).

Create your ad.

What do you want your ad to look like? It all depends on your original objective. If you're looking to increase the number of clicks to your website, Facebook's Ad Manager will suggest the Clicks to Website ad options.

This ad option is broken down into two formats: Links and Carousels. Essentially, this means that you can either display a single image ad (Links) or a multi-image ad (Carousel) with three to five scrolling images at no additional cost.

Once you decide between the two, you'll need to upload your images It's important to note that for each type of ad, Facebook requires users to adhere to certain design criteria. For single image ads, Facebook asks that users adhere to the following design recommendations:

- Text: 125 characters
- Ad Headline: 25 characters
- Image ratio: 1.91:1

- Image resolution (including CTA): 1080 x 1080 pixels

For multi-image ads -- also known as Carousel Ads -- Facebook provides the following design recommendations:

- Recommended image size: 1080 x 1080 pixels
- Image ratio: 1:1
- Text: 125 characters
- Headline: 40 characters
- Link description: 20 characters

Your image may not include more than 20% text. Keep in mind that these are the ad options for the "Traffic" objective. If you selected "boost your posts," you'd be presented with different ad options like the *Page Post Engagement: Photo ad*.

Once you select an ad type, the Ads Manager will prompt you to identify how you'd like to display your ad. The options they provide are as follows: Desktop News Feed, Mobile News Feed, and Desktop Right Column.

Monitor your ad's performance.

Once your ads are running, you'll want to keep an eye on how they're doing. To see their results, you'll want to look in two places: the Facebook Ad Manager and your marketing software. According to Facebook, these are some of the key metrics to look for (and their definitions):

42

- *Performance.* Can be customized to include metrics like results, reach, frequency and impressions
- *Engagement.* Can be customized to include metrics like Page likes, Page engagement and post engagement
- *Videos.* Can be customized to include metrics like video views and avg. % of video viewed
- *Website.* Can be customized to include metrics like website actions (all), checkouts, payment details, purchases and adds to cart
- *Apps.* Can be customized to include metrics like app installs, app engagement, credit spends, mobile app actions and cost per app engagement
- *Events.* Can be customized to include metrics like event responses and cost per event response
- *Clicks.* Can be customized to include metrics like clicks, unique clicks, CTR (click-through rate) and CPC (cost per click)
- *Settings.* Can be customized to include metrics like start date, end date, ad set name, ad ID, delivery, bid and objective

Regardless of which of these metrics you use to measure the success of your advertising efforts, you can find the data in the Ads Manager. As you analyse, you'll be thinking about your data in different ways depending on what information you need to get. This gives a view of performance across all campaigns. You'll find aggregate data that gives you a bird's eye view. Simply navigate to the ads manager and click Account Overview. From there, you'll be able to customize the metrics you want to see such as drill down time, ranges, and more.

The Campaign, Ad Set, or Ad Level

You can also get far more specific with your analysis by checking the performance of campaigns and even down to individual ads. This can help you figure out which messaging, audiences, and collateral are resonating the best. All you have to do is navigate to the Campaigns, Ad Sets, or Ads tabs next to Account Overview in the ads manager.

Reporting on Facebook ad performance.

You can receive custom reports via email as well. Navigate to Analyze and Report through the upper main menu. Choose Ads Reporting. Select *Create Custom Report*. Select and open a saved report. Choose *Save* As next to the save icon. Give your report a name and check Schedule Email. Follow the prompts to edit and confirm your reporting preferences.

.

Facebook and Instagram

This is relevant if you have an Instagram account. As you will see in the chapter on Instagram, it is entirely possible to link your Facebook ads to Instagram.

If you have already linked your Facebook page, Instagram account and Facebook advertising account through Business Manager, then you are ready to create instagram ads through the ads manager.

Facebook Ads

Get started

Go to Business Manager and use the Business Settings menu to navigate to Ad Accounts. Then click on the link to View Ad Account in Ads Manager. On the next screen, click the green Create Ad button on the top right. This will take you to the standard Ads Manager interface within your Business Manager to create a new ad. There, you can hover over the ad objectives to see which ones will allow you to create Instagram ads.

1: Select Your Objective - First off, select an objective that works with Instagram. Currently, you can choose from "Send people to your website," "Increase conversions on your website," "Get installs of your app" and "Get video views." Once you selected your objective, tell Ads Manager what you want to advertise and click Continue.

2: Choose Your Audience- Next, tell Ads Manager about the audience for your ad. If you have saved custom audiences, you can include or exclude them in the Custom Audiences field at the top.

3: Set Your Ad Budget and Scheduling- After you select your ad audience, set your ad budget and schedule when you want it to run. Facebook offers recommendations for bidding strategies with specific ad objectives. The ad objectives available for Instagram ads are as follows:

45

- Send people to your website: Optimize for link clicks, get charged for link clicks (CPC).

- Increase conversions on your website: Optimize for conversions, get charged for impressions.

- Get installs of your app: Optimize for app installs, get charged for impressions.

- Get video views: Optimize for video views, get charged for impressions.

You may want to experiment to see what optimization and pricing strategy works best for your ad campaign goals.

4: Create Your Ad- Depending on your ad objective, you first need to designate whether you want to use a single image or video or multiples. Make these selections, and then look below to see if Instagram is enabled as a placement. If it isn't, you need to change your selections. Now, select your ad creative (images or video). After you do, remember to scroll down and test what it will look like with each of your placements. You want to ensure they are properly optimized to look good.

With the above settings, the ad shown will be displayed on Instagram and in the Facebook news feed (desktop and mobile), Facebook right column (desktop only) and in Facebook's Audience Network (mobile banners on third-party apps outside of Facebook). However, you can also run an Instagram-only campaign. Just remove placements outside of Instagram.

If you're using Ads Manager without the Business Manager connections, you will have the option to select your Facebook page and add your Instagram account. Alternatively, you can also use your Facebook page to represent your business in your Instagram ad without connecting an Instagram account.

Note: When you connect your Instagram account to your ad, you'll get notifications about likes and comments on your Instagram ad in your mobile Instagram app. You may not get those notifications without the connection.

5: Run Your Ad and Review Insights

Once you configure your Instagram ad, click the green Place Order button at the bottom right of the page to submit it for review. Once approved by the Facebook advertising team, it will start to run, based on the schedule you specified. Visit your Ads Manager directly or via Business Manager to see the performance of your ad.

Remember to click through your campaign to see the breakdown of results by placement, if your ad is running on both Facebook and Instagram. Use the drop-down next to All Placement.

****

Chapter 3

Facebook Marketplace, Stores and Shops

Facebook marketplace, stores and shops (shops being a relatively new concept) are a vital addition to your social media marketing strategy. In addition to marketing your product you can also sell direct.

Many people use Shopify to sell goods on Facebook (plus sell goods on other sites). Shopify Inc.is a Canadian multinational e-commerce company headquartered in Ottawa, Ontario. It is also the name of its proprietary e-commerce platform for online stores and retail point-of-sale systems. Shopify offers online retailers a suite of services including payments, marketing, shipping and customer engagement tools. Shopify.co.uk.

There is a UK alternative to Shopify, this is Shopwired www.shopwired.co.uk which offers the same sort of services. Both Shopify and Shopwired charge monthly fees. There are others but the above are the most popular.

Facebook Marketplace

Facebook marketplace is a direct selling site. Utilised by 800 million people worldwide, Facebook Marketplace is hugely popular. Originally aimed at individuals, more and more businesses are now using this as a viable way to market and sell their products.

The marketplace is where users can easily snap a picture of a piece of property they don't want anymore and pop it on the marketplace with a price. Other users see the product they want and can then arrange payment with the poster or negotiate the price.

The platform is highly targeted, and therefore is ideal for businesses looking to provide a highly personalised service to customers, and with no listing fees it can prove to be a cost-effective e-commerce solution.

Facebook stores

In the past, e-commerce businesses would aim to push traffic from Facebook to their websites where they could convert to a customer. While we can still use Facebook to push traffic to our websites, it is a well-known truth that many users will not want to leave the platform. After all, if you are specifically looking for a product you would probably search for it on Google and you may only move from Facebook to an e-commerce website if something extra special caught your eye. More often than not if you did see something you might want to buy, you would think to come back and have a look later so you can keep scrolling and engaging on Facebook. In many instances you would probably forget to go back and check out the product in greater detail.

To resolve this, numerous Facebook shopping apps and services sprung up to allow users to buy products directly from a business Facebook page without ever having to leave the platform. The Facebook Shop Tab allows you to list your products and prices and sell directly on Facebook.

Add a store Section to your business page

Anyone with admin rights on your Facebook business page can create a Facebook store for you. First go to your business page. On your timeline you will see a number of features listed below your profile photo. At the bottom of the list you will find a button that says "add shop section". Click this button. When you click the button a pop-up will appear asking you if you want to create a store. Click the "add shop section" button that pops up here. You will be asked to confirm the currency you are working in, then agree to the merchant terms and policies and click continue. You can take a moment to read the merchant terms first, or come back to them later.

Set up the store

Make sure that you have your images and details ready. You will need a profile photo for your store. You will also need good quality product images. Facebook will allow you to use any relevant photo, but for the sake of selling your products it's best to make sure your images are clear and appealing.

The next pop-up will ask for business details. You will need to add your business e-mail address. There will be a small box that you can tick which says "use e-mail for custom service inquiries". It's a good idea to check this. What it does is send any inquiries posted to the page directly to you so that you can deal with them simultaneously.

The next pop up will ask you to add products to your shop. You can do this by filling in the simple form and uploading the product image. Don't worry if you are unsure about what to say here. You can always come back and edit your products later.

Set up your payment options

The Facebook store will ask you to set up payment options for any orders made through your store. You will choose how your money gets to you and what account it is paid into. Facebook works through a payment gateway called Stripe. They are compatible with most payment networks but you may want to consider setting up a Stripe account of your own if you don't already have one. There is a link in the payments set up area that will allow you set up your own Stripe account.

Finish Set Up

Once you've set up your store and your payment options choose the "finish setup" button to complete the process. You are now ready to start selling!

You can add more products with good descriptions and good quality images. Click the "Add Products" button to add new products to your site. You can then "Add photos". If you are happy with the photo's you've uploaded remember to click the "use photo" button. If you don't they won't be live on your site. You can give your customers more details on the variations your product comes in by clicking the "Edit variants" link in the product area. This is also where you will include shipping and payment information. You can choose the list view to see all of your products at once. This makes it really easy to keep your inventory up to date and remove anything that's out of stock.

Once you have your store set up it's time to let people know about it. Share with your groups and friends, set up a few Facebook ads and make sure that your Facebook business page is populated with posts and content that reflect your brand image and appeal to the interests of your target market. Then make sure you keep an eye on your store. Make sure you check for new orders, comments and queries every day to keep your customers happy.

Facebook Shops
Facebook has recently launched Facebook Shops, its brand-new e-commerce tool, aimed at small businesses. This is different to Facebook store. Having a 'shop' (a type of Facebook selling page) gets you selling directly through the platform. Facebook Shops may have come at the right time for struggling businesses hit by the coronavirus lockdown, keen to feel a bounce from any surge in online spend. And if you're ready to sell Facebook Shops might be a great place to start.

Selling on Facebook has the advantage of being simple to or go straight to a linked website

The simplicity of Facebook Shops means that small businesses can experiment with online retail and selling without going through a complicated set-up with a new provider. They can also use the tools they already know and trust. From Facebook itself to Instagram, WhatsApp and Messenger, all of these can (or will soon be) part of the experience for you and your customers.

Now read the summary of the main points from chapters 1, 2 and 3 overleaf.

****

In Summary

Using Facebook as a tool for social media marketing

We have seen that introducing Facebook into your marketing armoury will produce long term benefits for you and your business. Facebook has a massive reach and, with a small amount of hard work, you can set up your Business pages and utilise all the tools at your disposal to promote your business to the highest degree. There are a number of other sites which can also be utilised and be part of a strategy for social media marketing,, which we will cover in this book, but Facebook is the big one!

The benefits of using Facebook as a Social Media Marketing Tool

- Facebook puts businesses in touch with their customers, through its huge connectivity potential. It provides an ideal outlet for companies to reach out and generate a rapport with customers, old or new.
- Through Facebook, you can receive feedback on your products and services and also on your marketing campaign.
- Facebook pages can also generate traffic for your website. The more customers your page collects, the bigger your websites traffic.

- Facebook can also be used to increase the potential audience for your product and put you in a better position regarding sales.

- If you have a Facebook Group for your business that is exclusive to members that have purchased from you, then you can, for example, have special live videos that only they can access. This can be about product demonstrations or announcing new events and so on.

- Understanding how to maximise the reach of Facebook Ads has become a vital part of every social media marketing strategy. Paid advertising on Facebook seems to be one of the most immediate ways to impact the reach of your content.

- Facebook Marketplace, stores and shops (a relatively new concept) are a vital addition to your social media marketing strategy. In addition to marketing your product you can also sell direct.

****

Chapter 4

YOUTUBE

YouTube as A Social Media Marketing Tool

Having seen how (relatively) uncomplicated Facebook marketing can be, (once you have put in a lot of time and effort) we can now turn to the use of YouTube as a marketing tool. It is up to you whether you go down the YouTube route or decide to stick with Facebook for the moment. If you want wide social media coverage then you might want to develop a YouTube strategy alongside Facebook.

The big difference between YouTube and Facebook is that YouTube is entirely dependant on videos. A lot more time, effort and money, is spent on creating content. Getting your subscribers to watch your videos and engage with them, and follow your business, is a more complicated affair.

The benefits of YouTube to your business

Videos have become a very important part of a company's marketing strategy. People log into YouTube to search for their brands presence and go through the videos that they have uploaded. YouTube now has 3 million plus (growing all the time) viewers for its videos, and its reach is very wide indeed. If you have a large subscriber base then it is highly likely that your video will go viral.

You also have the option of redirecting people from your other social media accounts (such as Facebook) and further increase your chances of expanding your traffic and customer base.

It is also possible to have your company's own channel on YouTube where you can post videos of your products and services. Ideally, you should create a series of videos before allowing customers to access your channel.

Using YouTube Live

YouTube live, like Facebook live, allows you to host live videos on your channel. You can broadcast it live to your audience, if you so wish. It can be a demonstration video of your product, for example. The videos can be as informative as you want them to be which in turn can increase your sales.

Creating a YouTube channel

As with marketing generally, and as we saw with Facebook, when you use YouTube to promote your business you need to give a lot of thought about the end user and to whom you are targeting the video. As I have emphasised, building a channel can be a long, hard and expensive process. You should ask yourself:

- Why do I want or need to create a YouTube channel and for what purpose?

Obviously, as this book is about social media for marketing your aim will be to utilise YouTube for marketing your products.

- Is your goal to make money (there are easier ways!) or to showcase your product?
- Is it to build your brand and market your business?

Take a look at what else is on YouTube, to ensure that there is a chance to gain market share. Only when you are very clear about what it is you want should you consider YouTube as a marketing tool. Before we talk about the technicalities of producing a video we should look at the mechanics of creating a YouTube channel.

Get started

As stated, before you can promote your business on YouTube, and before you can build your YouTube audience, you need to start your YouTube channel! Getting started can always be a little bit daunting, but following the basic steps below will get you on the right track.

Create a Google Account

Go to accounts.google.com and click on "Create account". Fill in your details to create your Google Account. Click "Next step". You will be asked to verify your Google Account with a verification code sent to your phone. (It may take a few minutes to arrive). Once you've submitted that code and authenticated your account, you are ready to continue.

Navigate to the Google Apps launcher in the top right corner of the screen. Click on the Google Apps icon and then select the YouTube icon. You'll be taken directly to the YouTube homepage.

You will see a new screen where you will be asked who you wish to "Use YouTube as...". You can choose to "Create channel" using your Gmail details, or, in the case of a business account, you can select "Use a business or other name". These types of accounts can have multiple managers or owners — perfect for if you want your YouTube marketing to be a collaboration with several team members.

You will be asked to create a name for your Brand Account. Click "Create" to finish.

Fill out the details of your YouTube channel

Channel icon

1. First, change your channel icon. The icon is the small profile image that viewers will see over your channel cover art, on your videos, comments and so on.
2. Select "Customize channel".
3. Select the pencil button on your icon then click "Edit".
4. Select "Upload photo". You will then have the option to crop your image.
5. When you're ready, click "Done".

YouTube recommends using an image at 800 x 800 pixels. Your icon will be rendered into a circle for most of its appearances on YouTube. Keep that in mind when you choose and crop your image. It may take a few minutes for your new image to populate the channel icon, so don't worry if it doesn't appear immediately.

Channel art

Now it's time to customize your YouTube account by adding the perfect channel artwork. Personalizing your YouTube channel with channel art is another fantastic way to communicate who you are as a business and to stand out from the crowd.

Adding channel art :

Navigate back to YouTube using the Google Apps launcher in the top right corner of your screen (or by heading to YouTube.com).

1. From the YouTube homepage, click your icon in the top right corner
2. Go to "My channel".
3. Select "Customize channel."
4. Select "Add channel art".
5. Select "Upload photo".

YouTube recommends uploading your cover photo at 2560 x 1440 pixels with a maximum file size of 4MB. When you select an image, you will notice that YouTube provides a preview of how your channel art will appear on different devices (desktop,

TV, and mobile). You can choose to "Adjust the crop" to ensure your image looks perfect on each device.

Once you are ready, click "Select". With a customized icon and cover art, your YouTube channel will be taking shape and will boast some unique personality.

Channel description

The Next thing is to add a channel description.

1. Click on "Customize channel"
2. Navigate to "About"
3. Select the "Channel description" button.

Your YouTube channel description is your chance to tell people why you're here. The channel description is your bio. This is where people will come to find out who you are, what you stand for, and why they should watch your videos.

Your channel description can include useful details like your email address or your location. You could provide a link to your website or social media accounts, or connect with other relevant channels in the "Featured Channels" section.

But more importantly, your channel description should give people a reason to subscribe to you. Many of those getting started may not have their channel worked out. That's fine. As you begin to grow your channel, you'll discover your own creative flow and begin to develop a style of your own. Don't be afraid to adapt that style (or change it entirely) while you are getting started on YouTube.

This is the time to experiment, figure out what works, and uncover how you will bring value to your audience in a way no one else can.

Optimising your YouTube account

You have now completed some of the fundamental steps required to set up a YouTube channel. But we need to put in a bit more work optimise your YouTube content.

Add contact details

If you have set up a YouTube channel as a business or a brand, it is a good idea to include your contact details in the "About" section of your channel:

1. Navigate to "About", as above.

2. Scroll down to "Details". Add links

3. Allow your audience to quickly access the other marketing avenues of your business by adding links to your YouTube channel.

Go to your channel homepage. Select "Customize channel" and click the "cog" icon beneath your channel art.

"Channel Settings" will appear. Enable the "Customize the layout of your channel" option. Click "Save" and head back to your channel homepage.

Now that customizations have been enabled, you can find the "Edit links" option in the top right corner of your channel art. Click "Edit links" to be taken to the "About" page. Add links and choose how many will appear on your channel art.

You can add links to your website, email address, many different social media networks, merchandise providers and much more. Including these links provides opportunities for your viewers to become long-term followers of your brand. Keep those lines of communication open between your business and your audience!

Include a channel trailer

When you first setup a YouTube account, it can be easy to overlook the channel trailer. But in fact, your YouTube channel trailer could be one of the most influential methods of attracting new viewers. Channel trailers are auto-play videos that appear only for people who have not yet subscribed to your channel. Good channel trailers are typically short and to-the-point. They grab attention and give viewers a clear picture of who you are and what type of content you create.

Setting up a channel trailer for your YouTube account:

Make sure you have turned on channel customization in your "Channel settings".

1. Upload the video you want to be your channel trailer.
2. Navigate to "Customize channel".
3. Click the "For new visitors" tab.
4. Click on "Channel trailer".
5. Select your channel trailer and click "Save".

Upload your first video

When You've set up a YouTube channel, and got some content loaded, then the big moment has arrived — it is time to upload your first YouTube video!

1. Click on your icon in the top right corner of YouTube and select "Creator studio" from the drop-down menu.
2. Click on the "Upload" arrow in the top right.
3. This will take you to the YouTube Upload screen.

Before you upload your video, take note of the privacy settings:

- Public means your video will be accessible by everyone.
- Unlisted means only people with a link will be able to access your video.
- Private means only you can view the video.
- Scheduled allows you to arrange for the video to be released at a specified date. You may find this setting helpful in the future, when you are more experienced with your channel and start adhering to an upload schedule.

For now, It is recommended that you select "Private" (this is a good safety net to prevent viewers from seeing any mistakes you might make). If you accidentally upload the wrong video or forget to input some information, you can rectify the situation before anyone else views it.

Select your video and click "Upload".

On this next screen, you will be able to monitor your upload status. And while you are here waiting for the video to upload, you can perform a few essential steps to optimise your video.

Optimise your videos

There are four fundamental things that every single one of your YouTube videos must have: title, description, tags, and thumbnail. While you wait for the video to upload, you can fill in the title, description, and tags.

Title

Write a compelling title of around 70 characters in length. Be concise and descriptive about the video you are posting. Your titles should give potential viewers an insight into what your content is about, while also enticing them to click through.

Description

Include a video description to assist with YouTube's search and discovery system. Descriptions are a crucial source of information for YouTube's algorithm. Include clear and specific keywords to help YouTube and viewers understand what your video is about. Prioritise important information and keywords in the first few sentences. The video description is also a good place for calls to action or links to your website and social media accounts.

Tags

Use tags to improve the ranking and visibility of your video. Remember, keywords are king! Consider what words people might use if they were searching for videos like yours. Type in your keyword or phrase (a long-tail keyword) in the "Tags" field, then add a comma or hit enter to confirm. Never leave these three fields empty.

Optimizing your YouTube videos with effective titles, descriptions, and tags is crucial for working with YouTube's search algorithm. This is how viewers will be able to find your videos. Also, don't use misleading titles or tags in an attempt to get more views.

Thumbnail

Finally, we need to select a video thumbnail. Creating a custom thumbnail can be a great way of giving your channel a polished and professional look. But when you first set up a YouTube channel, you may find it easier to utilize the default thumbnails.

YouTube will supply you with several thumbnail suggestions for your video once it has finished uploading. You can use one of these, or create and upload your own thumbnail. Keep in mind that more than half of your audience will be viewing your channel on a mobile device. Be sure to choose a thumbnail that is clear to see on any device!

Make your video public

Now that your video has processed, we can preview it and made sure it has uploaded perfectly.

Select "Done".

It will tell you that "Your video is now ready at…" and provide you with the video URL. Click that link to review your video and its information. Once you're happy, navigate back to your "Creator studio" (via your icon in the top right corner).

Select "*Video manager*".

This is where you will always be able to see every single video that you upload. Select "Edit" on your video. If you ever want to make changes to your title, description, tags or privacy settings, you can do so here. Finally, change the privacy settings to "Public" so everyone can find and view your video.

From this screen, you can also add an end screen or annotations, write subtitles, add music or audio, or create other enhancements for your videos. These steps are all a little more complex. You may like to utilise them in the future, but you needn't worry about them too much for now.

Add the video to a playlist

Creating keyword-rich playlists is an effective way to improve your YouTube SEO and increase search traffic. These customized libraries will allow you to organize your videos based on topic, theme or other criteria. Playlists will help viewers find content, and ideally encourage them to watch more than one of your videos.

Think about the general categories of the things you are going to talk about in your videos. What topics are you going to cover? What is your niche?

Create a YouTube playlist

1. Under "Video manager" on the left side of your screen, select "Playlists".
2. Click the "New playlist" button and write a title.
3. Click "Create".
4. Like with individual videos, you should write a description for each playlist.
5. Select "Edit".
6. Select "Add a description".

Include relevant keywords and tell your audience what the videos in this playlist are about. If needed, you can also adjust the settings of your playlist. Simply click the "Playlist settings" button. Auto-add can make it easier to keep your YouTube playlists updated with the latest content.

A handy feature here is to "auto add" videos to a playlist. This setting allows you to define rules for videos based on words that appear in the title, description or tags of your video. If your video meets one of these rules, it will be automatically added it to the playlist.

Promoting your YouTube channel

You've put in the time and effort to set up a YouTube channel with all the bells and whistles. You need to make sure people can find it! Below are ways to promote your YouTube content and improve your online visibility.

Share on social media

One of the first things you should do once you've set up a YouTube channel is to tell people about it on social media. Share your videos on every social media platform imaginable. Facebook might be the best video sharing platform, but there are plenty of other spaces to consider.

If your business is on Twitter, LinkedIn, Google+ or other social channels, promote your YouTube channel there too! Most of all, the goal is to cross-post your content wherever possible for maximum visibility.

Social bookmarking sites, such as PearlTrees or StumbleUpon, can also be excellent referral sources for your content. They create social signals that can help improve your search rankings.

Send an email

Email direct marketing is one of the most effective means of connecting directly with your audience. Send out an email to your email list to let them know you have set up a YouTube channel. Send emails whenever you post a new video and encourage readers to subscribe to the channel. Email marketing is a quick, easy and personal form of communication. Send out an email in a matter of minutes, and you could increase your number of views within hours.

Embed your videos

Embedding your videos and sharing buttons are two ways to get your content in front of more people. Embed your videos wherever you can. Websites, blog posts, forums, social platforms, chat rooms — the more SEO backlinking you create, the more likely your content is going to be found.

Remember that adding video content to your blogs and websites will increase user engagement. These shares can drive your channel's traffic until it creates organic search traffic and maximizes your reach.

Use Google AdWords

Investing in Google AdWords will allow you to promote your channel to YouTube viewers with PPC (pay-per-click) advertisements. This is an effective advertising strategy that can accelerate your viewership and get your content seen by more people. Simply connect your YouTube channel to a Google AdWords account, create an ad, set a budget, and set the target audience. You can choose to create in-stream ads (which appear before or after your video) or in-display ads (which appear alongside the video or on the search page).

> ### *Videos-the practical side*
> *Having looked at videos and discussed setting up your YouTube channel, we need to look at the practical side of videos, i.e. how to make one and what equipment you might need. One thing we do know, there is no perfect format for a video. There is no ideal length. The video you make, as a business, will be tailored around your product. The only way to understand whether your video is working or not is to make one and pay attention to YouTube analytics. You can then refine your video as you go.*

The recommended format for a video

OPENING: This will be a quick introduction that will tell people what it is they are about to see in the video. Whatever your product is make sure that you get a shot of that product in the first 10 seconds or so. End the opening with a joke or other witty comment which will lead the viewer into the intro music.

TITLE/INTRODUCTION: This will be an introductory sequence with some music and the title. Remember, with music and the title you are trying to evoke the overall feel of the show. This should be short, around 5-10 seconds.

THE CONTENT: When showing the content you can slow down and get into the main show. The actual pacing is wholly determined by the subject matter.

THE END CARD: This continues the branding that has already been established and is a chance to send people to your website and further see your product. You can also send people to another video if you have one. Once you have made and launched a few videos you can then go to Video retention Analytics and see how things are working. The Analytics will tell you when people are looking at your video, how often and at what point they leave your video.

(See below for more about YouTube Analytics).

What equipment do you need to make a video?

If you are going to make a video, you need to know about the equipment that it takes to make a good quality show. One thing that we do know is that camera technology is advancing at a rapid rate. The main message, rather than doing hours of research is to find something that works for you and get on and make your video.

What you will need depends very much on the kind of video that you are going to produce. You can use an iPhone. With an iPhone you can purchase a few accessories and then you are in a position to produce high quality videos. However, while smartphones certainly are a good first step, they lack many of the features that will take your channel's production qualities to the next level.

Ideally you want something that can capture great quality video and audio, automatically keep your face in focus, and be small enough to carry around. You might even want livestreaming capabilities in order to share your musings in real-time.

Using a camera

One good website which will go into the specifications of numerous cameras is: www.techradar.com/best/best-youtube-camera. This site indicates prices from around £700 to £1500 and above. While your needs will vary slightly depending on the kind of videos you're looking to shoot, there are five main features that you should look for in a YouTube camera:

1. Articulating screen

Whether it flips out to the side or pivots up to the top, an articulating screen is a godsend when trying to film yourself. By giving you a live preview of the shot composition, exposure and focus, it helps you get the basics right so you can concentrate on other aspects of your video.

2. Good autofocus

Manual focus has its place in filmmaking, but to keep everything as simple and straightforward as possible it pays to pick a camera with great video autofocus. Face and/or eye tracking helps if you tend to move around a lot in your videos, as the focus will adjust itself automatically to compensate.

3. Built-in stabilization

Filming on the hoof can result in shaky, hard to watch footage. Thankfully a lot of modern cameras come with image stabilization (optical, electronic or a combination of the two) to automatically compensate for motion. Some, it should be noted, do it much better than others. Alternatively, a gimbal can stabilize pretty much any camera, at the cost of adding bulk.

4. Audio options

A camera's built-in microphone can record sound – but using an external microphone will vastly improve clarity and likely cut down on unwanted ambient noise. Check potential buys for mic inputs and a hot shoe for mounting mics. You might want to consider headphone sockets too: they allow you to monitor audio levels while recording.

5. Livestreaming options

This might not be vital for those making videos to upload after filming and editing, but for anyone who wants to broadcast live, it's well worth checking to see if a potential camera supports YouTube livestreaming. It's not just smartphones and webcams anymore – more and more cameras are coming with the technology built-in.

Online advice

You will have deduced by now that actually making a video can be quite a complex affair. However, there is a lot of very useful advice online which you can access which will make the process a whole lot easier. A very useful website is:

www.techsmith.com/blog/make-youtube-video.

Analysing your performance

As with Facebook, YouTube has an analytics function and it also has Collaboration with Other YouTube users. Taken together and used correctly, these functions can increase both your engagement with users and also your revenue.

YouTube Analytics

Although at first, YouTube Analytics might seem difficult to understand, comprising graphs and charts, it is simple once you know how. When you have started your first channel and load up the Analytics dashboard, there won't be much there. Once you have been able to get at least a few hundred views, you can then start checking into your analytics to see what has been going on. Typically, YouTube Analytics data is several days behind what is happening so bear in mind that what you are viewing isn't the full picture. There is, however, a real time section in the dashboard which will give you statistics on the last 24 hours of views.

Watch time

Watch time is defined as the number of minutes that a viewer spends watching a video. For YouTube, a channel with a higher watch time means more revenue because the channel can clearly hold a viewer's attention. One way to improve your watch time is to experiment with tweaking your video format and quality of the content. The goal is to make your video more useful, and watchable.

Other useful metrics

There are a number of other metrics which are important tools to analyse performance:

Subscriber to view ratio-this is an indication of how engaging your videos are to your subscriber base;

Video views in the first 24 to 48 hours-this indicates how engaged your subscribers are, and how quickly your video begins ranking in search;

Traffic sources-how are people finding your video? if you know, then you can try to exploit that source and increase traffic further;

Traffic locations-What is the location of most areas of your traffic? is your content resonating more with a specific country? If your content is resonating with a non-English speaking country for example then it might be worth getting your video translated into the language of that country.

If you go to the 'Overview' section of the Analytics dashboard then you can see which videos have the most viewings, both total and daily views. This will help you to build up a picture of how you are doing overall.

Collaborating with other YouTube channels

A collaboration is when two YouTubers come together to make a video. They typically create separate videos for each channel and promote each others videos on their social media outlets. This can, if achieved, create a lot of growth by exposing you to a new audience.

If a YouTuber has an engaged subscriber base, collaborating with them means that you are exposed to their viewers, who then might subscribe to your channel.

How to find collaborations

In the first instance, actually locating partners to collaborate with can be difficult. The key is creating organic relationships with other YouTubers in your genre. YouTube is a social platform which means that you always have to be networking in order to create and sustain relationships. This means commenting on other YouTuber channels and videos and following other YouTubers on Instagram etc. Networking on You Tube is something that has to be done daily if you want to see results!

Advertising on YouTube

The beauty of YouTube videos is that you can generate revenues by merely making and uploading a video. YouTube runs ads on your videos and they pay you a percentage of what they make. This is usually the easiest and fastest way of making money!

The YouTube ad system is driven by the concept of CPM, which stands for Cost per Mile or Cost Per Thousand Views. Individual views aren't worth much but advertisers are willing to pay for them in batches of a thousand.

If you are familiar with Google's AdSense system, you should have an idea of how YouTubes AD system works. Advertisers set up AD campaigns targeting certain keywords, interests and demographics and place auction style bids for ad placements.

Now read a summary of the main points from Chapter 4 overleaf.

****

In Summary

Using YouTube as a Tool for Social Media Marketing

- It is up to you whether you go down the YouTube route or decide to stick with Facebook for the moment. If you want wide social media coverage then you might want to develop a YouTube strategy alongside Facebook.

- The big difference between YouTube and Facebook is that YouTube is entirely dependant on videos. A lot more time and effort, and money, is spent on creating content. Getting your subscribers to watch your videos and engage with them, and follow your business, is a more complicated affair.

- YouTube live, like Facebook live, allows you to host live videos on your channel. You can broadcast it live to your audience, if you so wish. It can be a demonstration video of your product, for example. The videos can be as informative as you want them to be which in turn can increase your sales.

- There is no perfect format for a video. There is no ideal length. The video you make, as a business, will be tailored around your product. The only way to understand whether your video is working or not is to make one and pay attention to YouTube analytics. You can then refine your video as you go.

  - If you are going to make a video, you need to know about the equipment that it takes to make a good

- quality show. One thing that we do know is that camera technology is advancing at a rapid rate. The main message, rather than doing hours of research is to find something that works for you and get on and make your video.
- The beauty of YouTube videos is that you can generate revenues by merely making and uploading a video. YouTube runs ads on your videos and they pay you a percentage of what they make. This is usually the easiest and fastest way of making money!

****

Chapter 5

LINKEDIN

Using LinkedIn as A Social Media Marketing Tool

LinkedIn

LinkedIn is different to the social media sites covered so far, (Facebook and YouTube). It is, however, still a very powerful tool for marketing your business and worth looking into.

With over 300 million users, (at the last count but growing all the time) LinkedIn is a social network geared toward career professionals. It's a very effective platform for promoting your business. It can be used for finding a job or for freelance work. Importantly, it can also be used for connecting with joint venture partners.

If you have a business that caters to other businesses or have a business in which networking for partners or clients is important, you should most definitely have a profile on LinkedIn. Like other forms of internet marketing, marketing a business on LinkedIn is an inexpensive way to gain exposure.

Overview of LinkedIn

LinkedIn is a social network specifically designed for career and business professionals to connect. Unlike other social networks in which you might become "friends" with anyone and everyone, LinkedIn is about building strategic relationships. *Thus, the number of connections is less important than the type of connections.*

The site boasts members from just about every country and every industry imaginable. LinkedIn has some advertising, but it's not as invasive as other networking sites.

On LinkedIn, you start by connecting with those you know and who know you, and through them build a larger network for the purpose of gaining resources, finding freelance work or clients, and building alliances and partnerships.

How to Use LinkedIn

LinkedIn has its own platform and system different from other networks, but learning how to use LinkedIn is no more difficult than learning how to use any other social networking site. As with all other social networking sites, you start by creating a personal LinkedIn account and profile.

Getting started

In order to get started with LinkedIn, you'll need to create an account. Once your account is set up, you can then start adding others to your network and building a powerful tool you can use for your benefit.

Step-by-step instructions for creating a LinkedIn login.

1. Open your Web browser and go to LinkedIn.com.
2. Complete the information in the Join LinkedIn Today (right) area of the page
3. Type your First Name in the First Name box.
4. Type your Last Name in the Last Name box.
5. Type a valid email address where you receive email.
6. Select a Password for your account. The password needs to be at least six letters. It's a good idea to use both lowercase and capital letters along with at least one number or special character to create a strong password. Don't leave any blank spaces.
7. Click **Join Now**. This will move you to the next LinkedIn screen.

You're ready to proceed to the next step in creating a LinkedIn login. The next step in creating a LinkedIn login is to provide your employment status and location information.

On the next screen that displays:

Select your current work status. Selections are: Employed, A business owner, Looking for work, Working independently or A student. Your selection determines the fields you see next.

If you selected **Employed** the remaining fields you'll need to complete will be Company, Job Title, Country and post Code where you live.

If you select **A business owner** (which you probably are if you want to use LinkedIn to market your business) you'll be asked for the name of your business (Company Name), the Industry to which your business belongs, Country and post Code where you live.

This may not be relevant if you are seeking to market your business, but if you selected **Looking for work** or **Working independently**, you'll be asked to provide the Industry in which you're seeking work (or currently working), Country and post code where you live

If you select **A student** you'll be asked to provide information on the name of your College/University (when you begin typing, you'll see a list of schools that matched what you typed. You can either select one or finish typing), the dates you attended (starting and expected year of graduation - you must make a selection), your Field of Interest (you must make a selection so choose the closest fit), Country and post code where you live.

In all cases, your post code is kept private, but your region is displayed. LinkedIn will not ask you for your street address unless you order a premium account after you've established your login.

Re-check your selections. When you are ready, click Continue to go to the next step in the process of setting up a LinkedIn login.

The next step in creating a LinkedIn login is optional. You can start building your LinkedIn network by importing contacts from your email address book. After you've finished providing your employment status and location information from the previous step in creating your login, the *See Who You Already Know* on LinkedIn window will display.

The purpose of this window is to import contacts from your email address contacts to see if any of the email addresses you have stored match LinkedIn members. You can choose from a number of addresses, such as hotmail and Gmail.

Other

If you chose **Other** a selection list becomes available in which you can select from many other email services for your contacts. In all cases, you'll need to log in to your email account so LinkedIn can fetch your stored email addresses from your address book.

This above step is optional. If you don't want to use this feature, click the **Skip this step** link near the bottom of the screen. Just because LinkedIn isn't able to match up a LinkedIn account with an email address in your address book, doesn't mean that person isn't on LinkedIn. It's possible that they signed up with a different email account.

Once you've either gone through the email address or skipped over it, a confirmation screen displays to let you know that a confirmation email has been sent to the email account you just registered with LinkedIn. If LinkedIn recognized your email provider, a button will be available that you can click to go directly to your (Webmail) email provider, where you can log in and receive the confirmation message sent by LinkedIn.

You may receive LinkedIn's confirmation immediately or it could take several minutes. Once you receive the message, all you need to do is:

1. Click the link in LinkedIn's confirmation message.
2. Log in to LinkedIn with the login you just created.
3. Start using LinkedIn!

LinkedIn offers a tremendous opportunity to share your business with prospective partners, clients, and customers. Whether you use LinkedIn to network for your business or to look for freelance work, your LinkedIn profile is crucial to attracting contacts. Once you've established a LinkedIn login (set up an account) and you understand how LinkedIn works, you'll want to create an effective LinkedIn profile.

Creating a LinkedIn Profile

By now you will have created your LinkedIn account). This is free but you can also upgrade to one of the paid LinkedIn subscriptions: Premium Career, Business Plus, LinkedIn Learning, Sales Navigator (three levels), and Recruiter Lite. Using just the basic free services is sufficient for many business owners and gets you features such as:

- Having a professional profile of skills, experiences, and more
- Limited insight into who's viewed your profile

- Ability to see 100 profiles per search
- Ability to save three searches

Upgrading increases some of these features, such as seeing more information about who's viewed your profile, the number of profiles per search, and the number of searches. Plus, upgrades can include additional features such as InMail credits, which allows you to message people who are not connected to you, and premium filters, which make searching faster and easier.

Once you sign up for a LinkedIn account, either free or paid, you can create your own professional profile. Remember, this is a professional-minded website, so it's important that information in your profile represents your business or career.

Some of the items you can add to a profile include the basics of your CV, a summary of yourself, your contact information, links to your website or blog, your previous employers, published books, and notable projects. Don't forget to add a professional picture, as people are reluctant to connect with someone without a photo.

Once your profile is complete, you can publish it and start looking for "connections." A connection is a person that you know or would like to know. Essentially, the idea is to create as many direct connections as you can by adding people within your own professional circle and branching out to include their connections. Your connections can also provide introductions to other professionals you might be interested in meeting.

While LinkedIn makes it easy to fill out your profile, there are a few things to keep in mind as you go through the process. Unlike Facebook and other social media platforms that involve social, daily life and entertainment aspects, as well as business, LinkedIn is exclusively geared toward professionals. Nearly half of LinkedIn members are decision-makers for their companies, so you'll want to make your best impression.

Unless LinkedIn members know you already, they're more likely to find you based on a search of skills or industries. Because of this, you need to consider the skills and industry you want to be known in, and determine the best keywords to describe them. For example, if you have a small non-fiction publishing business, your keywords and phrases might be 'non-fiction, publishing, books'.

As you build your LinkedIn profile, you'll use your key phrases in the various sections that describe your skills and experience.

The importance of key words

One of the biggest factors in search engine optimisation is the keyword. This is how people find you. If you want any sort of content to be visible on the internet you need to have enough relevant keywords in it. This applies equally to your linkedIn profile.

The first thing you need to do is to use LinkedIn's search feature to look up relevant keywords for your niche and create a list. If you are involved in sales then for certain the words 'sales' and 'selling' have to appear.

The next step is to use these relevant keywords one by one and see how you rank in the search results. The further down you are in the results, the more improvements your profile needs. You might want to look up the profiles of the people who are high up on the list and take a note of the key areas. You can then go to your own profile and edit it.

Components of a LinkedIn Profile

A LinkedIn profile has several main components, plus the ability to add more if they're a fit with your skills and experience. Along with adding text content, you can also add links, documents, video, and a presentation to most sections.

Title: This part of your profile appears directly under your name. You can write a sentence summary, but often it's more effective to have a list of skills you're known for. Make sure you use your keywords and phrases to make it easy for potential connections to find you.

Summary: Your summary allows you to create a free-form description of your experience, expertise, and your objectives. There are two sections: 1) Professional Experience & Goals, and 2) Specialties. Focus this area not just on how great you are in your business, but instead on the benefits you offer. For example, don't just say, "I'm a freelance copywriter." Instead say, "I write copy that makes your business stand out from the crowd."

Tips for a good summary include:
- Make sure this area is well written using proper grammar and is typo-free.
- Use short paragraphs with just one or two sentences each.
- Do use your key phrases wherever appropriate.
- Try to keep your summary punchy, to the point and interesting.

List each specialty on a separate line and make it easy for people to see your skills by using a bulleted list.

Experience: LinkedIn allows you to create an online CV with your current and previous work experience. This can be useful in business if you are freelance and looking to promote yourself. Be honest, but don't be afraid to work in your key phrases in this area. Also keep in mind, that if you are currently active in more than one position (I.e. you offer consulting services part-time, but you also work for a bank), the position you list with the most recent start date will appear at the top of your employment list.

Use your official job title, such as managing director, (if you have one) but include your key phrases when outlining your experiences and successes. Keep your descriptions easy to read, using short sentences and pressing the enter key to insert a line break. Use asterisks or + signs to make a bulleted list. This is another area where you want to focus on the benefits of your experience, not just the experience itself.

The goal is to keep your readers engaged so they don't want to leave right away without finding out more about you.

Education. Since your LinkedIn profile is an online CV, this area is important if formal education is expected to be related to your work. Education can be impressive to some, so don't leave this out.

Additional Information. Just as it is with a paper CV, consider adding information that highlights your abilities related to your work. You can add your interests, personal information and contact details. Just don't list anything you wouldn't want a potential customer to know about or you wouldn't want to be public information. Keep your LinkedIn profile professional.

Improve Your Profile. Once you have your basic profile filled out, you can see what other features you can fill in by clicking the "Improve Your Profile" option. You'll get a list of things you can add such as:

- Projects
- Publications
- Languages
- Volunteer experience
- Honors and Awards
- Certificates

After Your Profile Is Complete

Don't make the mistake of seeking connections before your profile is complete. At the very least have a professional picture, summary, experience and education completed before reaching out to others to connect. Start your network by connecting with people you know and/or know you. Through them, you can reach out to others. At this point, you can also work on endorsements and recommendations.

Skills and Endorsements: You can add your skills to this section during the initial profile set up, but at some point, you'll want endorsements. LinkedIn actually helps you with this by asking your connections to endorse you for skills you have listed. As a way to encourage endorsements, you should endorse others for their skills as well.

Recommendations: After you have established a LinkedIn profile and have built up some LinkedIn connections in your network, ask for recommendations from people who are familiar with your professional skills. The right recommendations can help your profile stand out and can lead to landing clients. One of the best ways to get recommendations is to first write a LinkedIn recommendation for someone. During that process, the person you recommend will be asked to write one for you. To see how your LinkedIn profile looks to the public, click the link next to **Public Profile** on the Edit My Profile page.

Keep Your LinkedIn Profile up to Date

Creating a LinkedIn profile is an easy undertaking, but it requires planning and nurturing to realize results. Since this online CV is available around the clock to potential connections and even possible clients, you will want to make sure it shines.

Building a Business brand on LinkedIn

As we have seen, LinkedIn is an important part of your social media marketing mix. Consider it a primary lead generation and connection-creating tool that also acts as an essential business branding tool.

LinkedIn Ads

Like most of the social media sites, LinkedIn offers users (at a price) the facility to post Ads on the site. The below outline gives you an overview of LinkedIn Ads and how they work, and the possible benefits to your company. LinkedIn Ads works on a bidding system, and lets you show an ad to the audience of your choice. You can target specific audiences, and control your budget. This is all similar to what we've seen on other platforms. The ads themselves, though, have slightly different formats from what we're used to.

First things first, if you are going to advertise on LinkedIn, your company needs to have a LinkedIn company page to publish content. To create ads on LinkedIn, go to your campaign manager. From there, click "Create Campaign" in the top right-hand corner. For step by step instructions to create a campaign go to: https://business.linkedin.com/Ads

There are other useful websites such as:

www.searchenginejournal.com/social-media/linkedin-advertising-guide

LinkedIn ad types

Like other social advertising platforms, LinkedIn advertising offers you a variety of ad types and formats to play with. And, like other platforms, you should be selecting your ad format based on the overall action you want to drive. Across all their offerings, LinkedIn advertising supports brand awareness, website visits, engagement, video views, lead generation, site conversions, and job applications.

LinkedIn sponsored content

Sponsored content ads look and feel native to the LinkedIn platform. These are the ads that appear to be "boosted" posts from a company's own feed. Your ads manager can create a typical post with a headline, image and link to sponsor. Or you can create carousel ads, video ads, and lead generation ads that appear in the same "boosted" format.

LinkedIn text ads

LinkedIn text ads are the closest to Google or Bing search ads that you can get on the platform. LinedIn text ads operate on a familiar pay-per-click or impression basis, and they're featured in the sidebar.

LinkedIn Sponsored InMail

Marketers or sales teams can curate a list of contacts to send personalized messages to. The content of the messages is largely up to you – you want to invite prospects to events or even attempt to generate an inbound call.

LinkedIn programmatic display ads

LinkedIn joined the fray of programmatic offerings, which is great news for B2B advertisers who rarely have good options for targeting. With these display ads, you can target the largest professional audience based on intent or personas. In terms of creativity, they are your run-of-the-mill display ads. Marketers can choose their preferred demand-side platform or trading desk and buy inventory through open or private auctions.

LinkedIn dynamic ads

Dynamic ads are basically as personalized as you can get with your LinkedIn advertising. Advertisers can choose to promote job postings, content downloads, their own company page, or drive traffic to a website via spotlight ads, which also appear on the newsfeed.

This ad type also has set templates and auto-translation options to make personalizing the ad easy for you.

LinkedIn advertising costs

As on other platforms, LinkedIn advertising costs are determined by your bids and budgets. This means that your overall ad spend will vary depending on your business and your goals, because this determines the types of ads that you choose for your campaigns and the budgets that you set. Typically, LinkedIn advertising starts at £3-4 per click, however, this can really vary. Be prepared to spend £4-6 per click. You can set your own budgets, so there is no need for a surprise overspend.

LinkedIn advertising targeting options

The targeting on this social platform is better than most. It's regularly updated and thorough, because professionals like to talk about all of their promotions and achievements. Members contribute their own job titles, company names, seniority, professional interests, and more. With over 300 million members, it's extremely likely your LinkedIn ads are going to Audience options. LinkedIn ads come with exhaustive options for targeting, which means that you're able to make sure your ads are getting served to the right people. If you are interested in testing the effectiveness of an ad against different audiences, you can save your audience as a template to build on later.

To set up your LinkedIn advertising targeting, start with the basics first: language and location. You can choose a permanent geolocation as specified in user profiles, i.e., "The Greater London Area," or shorter-term location based on IP address. Once you've determined the language and location, you can narrow down your audience based on these targeting options available.

Targeting by company

This is especially useful. If targeting a specific company isn't right for your strategy, you can still use this targeting option to narrow down your audience.

Company connections: LinkedIn allows you to target first-degree connections of selected companies – if they have over 500 employees.

Company followers: This selection will let you reach your company page followers.

Industries: Based on the primary industry listed on company pages, you can reach LinkedIn members employed in those industries.

Names: Reach employees based on the company name listed on their profiles.

Size: Based on the number of employees listed on a company profile, you can reach employees who work at companies of a certain size.

Demographic

This is much simpler: Add members to your audience that are of a certain age or gender, which is inferred from their profile.

Education

LinkedIn Ads lets you reach members based on their degrees, fields of study and the institution they attended.

Functions or skills: You can build an audience composed of tasks in their job positions or skills listed in their profiles. The skills can also be gleaned from endorsements from connections.

Seniorities, titles, or experience: Reach LinkedIn members with a certain level of seniority, a job title, or years of experience listed on their page.

Interests

LinkedIn introduced interest-based targeting recently. Now, you can include users who have joined groups around certain interests – like brand marketing or digital advertising – and people with interests that align with your business.

Now read a summary of the main points from Chapter 5 overleaf.

****

In Summary

Using LinkedIn as a tool for social media marketing

- LinkedIn is different to the social media sites covered so far, Facebook and YouTube. It is, however, still a very powerful tool for marketing your business and worth looking into..
- LinkedIn is a social network geared toward career professionals. It's a very effective platform for promoting your business
- On LinkedIn, you start by connecting with those you know and who know you, and through them build a larger network for the purpose of gaining resources, finding freelance work or clients, and building alliances and partnerships.
- One of the biggest factors in search engine optimisation is the keyword. This is how people find you. If you want any sort of content to be visible on the internet you need to have enough relevant keywords in it. This applies equally to your LinkedIn profile.
- Creating a LinkedIn profile is an easy undertaking, but it requires planning and nurturing to realize results. Since this online CV is available around the clock to potential connections and even possible clients, you will want to make sure it shines.
- Think of your social media marketing mix. Consider it a primary lead generation and connection-creating tool

that also acts as an essential business branding tool. Business entrepreneurs and professionals recognize LinkedIn's strategic marketing value as well as in other aspects of branding. And timing is everything.

■ Like most of the social media sites, LinkedIn offers users (at a price) the facility to post Ads on the site. LinkedIn Ads works on a bidding system, and lets you show an ad to the audience of your choice. You can target specific audiences, and control your budget. This is all similar to what we've seen on other platforms.

****

Chapter 6

TWITTER

Twitter as A Social Media Marketing Tool

> **Twitter for business**
>
> *Twitter is one of the world's most popular social media platforms with over 335 million users (at 2021 but changes upwards all the time). Many businesses use Twitter to reach and connect with their customers. As with all social media networks, You need to consider if a twitter account will benefit your business. Are your competitors using it? How do other people in your industry use it? What success are your peers having on Twitter?*

Benefits of Twitter for business

There are a number of advantages that using twitter can bring to a business:

- **Reach a wide audience:** Twitter has a large user base, which could include your potential customers. Using hashtags can help you reach an audience interested in a particular topic or in a particular location.

- **Deliver customer service:** The platform allows direct two-way communication with your customers. Because it's a public interaction, if you do it well it shows your business in a positive light

- **Brand identity:** Being on Twitter can help communicate your brand ethos and personality. This should help your business appeal to your target audience.

- **Feedback:** Twitter can be a useful resource for gathering feedback from customers.

- **Cost:** It is free of charge to set up a Twitter account. While paid ads are available, many businesses see benefits from organic posts and interactions.

Challenges of Twitter for business

It's important be aware of the downsides of Twitter for businesses:

- **Resources:** Maintaining a presence on Twitter requires a time commitment. It's also important that the staff looking after the account have the right skills and training. This applies to all of the social media platforms.

- **Criticism**: Customers could complain publicly about product or services.

- Negative comments can reflect badly on your business. However dealing with complaints well can have a positive impact on your reputation.
- **Time sensitive:** Unless you tweet at the right time, when your followers are online, your tweets could easily be missed. Again, as with other platforms, timing is crucial.
- **Spam:** Be wary of spam accounts on Twitter. In particular, do not click on suspicious links from users you don't know. This has become more of a problem recently.
- **Limitations:** You are restricted by Twitter's 280 character limit. It can take time to learn how to communicate effectively with brevity. Once again, as you use the platform you will learn these skills.

Set up and run a Twitter account for business

If you've decided that running a Twitter account will benefit your business, set up a profile that communicates your brand. Plan regular, relevant content and interact with your audience.

How to Create a New Twitter Account

To join Twitter from a web browser or mobile app:

1. Open a web browser, go to the Twitter website, and click **Sign Up**. On the Twitter app, tap **Create account**.
2. Enter your **name**, **phone number** or **email**, and **date of birth**, then select **Next**.
3. Enable or disable the **Track where you see Twitter content across the web** option, then select **Next**.

4. Select **Sign up** if your name, phone number or email, and date of birth are correct.
5. Enter the **verification code** from text or email, then select **Next**.
6. Enter a new **Password**, then select **Next**.

How to Complete Your Twitter Profile

At this point, you can go to the Twitter home page to access your account, or you can continue the set up process. Before you start following and tweeting, it's a good idea to finish setting up your profile so that it looks compelling enough for people to follow you back. You know, consider changing your Twitter background to grab some attention.

Choosing your name and customising your profile

When selecting your Twitter name you should choose your business name if it is available. Once you've selected your name, you should customise your profile. This will involve adding your introductory bio, which briefly explains your business.

Complete your profile by adding your company location and web address. You should add a profile picture. This could be your company logo or an individual if it is for a member of staff. Finally you can choose a cover image. You might want to use something that strengthens your brand or represents what your business does. When starting out on Twitter you may want to follow like-minded people or organisations. These could be:

• competitors

- suppliers
- other local businesses
- industry experts
- influencers
- customers

You will find that these people will often follow you back. When you follow someone their tweets will appear on your timeline creating your online community. You can also raise awareness of your Twitter channel by including your Twitter name on your website, business literature and email signature.

Posting content

A post on Twitter (a tweet) may consist of up 280 characters of text, an image, GIF, video, poll or link. You may choose to tweet a few times a week or up to several times a day. It may be useful to create a **content plan** to help you decide when and what to post. Remember to focus on content that your audience will find **useful, relevant and engaging**. A smaller portion of your tweets can be sales-focused with a call to action. It may be worth paying for extra promotion on your sales focused tweets. Twitter's **media studio tool** can help you easily share media content like images and videos.

Twitter interactions

An interaction is when someone engages with your Twitter channel - interactions include:

Follow - someone who follows you on Twitter. Your tweets will appear on their timeline.

Retweet - when another Twitter user shares one of your tweets with their followers. This does not necessarily mean that they are endorsing your content, but it does suggest that you have posted something that is of interest to them and their followers.

Mention - when someone else includes your Twitter name in a tweet that they send. Mentions could occur if someone is referring to you or asking you a question.

Like - when someone likes your tweet. This can be an acknowledgment or support of your message. It can be used as a response from a person or organisation that you have mentioned in a tweet. It is a positive interaction and should be measured in this way. There are no set rules for who should be using Twitter, or indeed how to use Twitter. Some digital marketing experts refer to Twitter etiquette but it's about finding out what works for your business. The basic communication elements remain - be polite, be courteous, deliver clear and concise messages, and respond to questions people ask you.

Hashtags

Twitter was the first social network to use hashtags as a search feature. By placing the # symbol at the start of a keyword or

108

phrase you can search for tweets relating to it. For example if you are looking for information on starting a business you could search the hashtag **#startup**.

When you are logged into your Twitter profile you will see the top trending hashtags in real time. These can often be specific to a breaking news story, a celebrity or popular television programme. Use hashtags in your tweets to help them be seen by people interested in a particular topic. You can also start your own hashtags for events and campaigns.

Twitter polls

You can use polls to ask questions to your Twitter audience. Polls allow you to add four answer options. Your poll's duration defaults to 1 day, but you can change this. The minimum amount of time for a poll is 5 minutes, and the maximum is 7 days. How each individual votes in the poll is not shared publicly.

To create a poll you compose a tweet and select 'poll'. You then add your question and edit the choices. Once you hit 'tweet' the poll will start. By using Twitter polls you can increase engagement by letting customers interact and engage with your brand. You can also use the data collected as useful market research.

Tools to manage Twitter

There are a number of tool available to help you manage your business' presence on Twitter. These tools allow you manage tasks that include, scheduling tweets, monitoring interactions and saving searches. Some examples include:

- Tweetdeck (Twitter's own free tool)
- HootSuite (third-party, paid but offers a free trial)
- Buffer (third-party, free basic account with options to pay for more features)

Twitter Ads-running an advertising campaign on Twitter

Advertising on Twitter enables you to promote individual tweets or entire campaigns dedicated to specific objectives. Businesses can choose between eight different objectives including app installs, video views, and website conversions and set audience targeting criteria for each ad campaign they create. To expand your reach and grow your follower list on Twitter, consider supplementing your organic efforts with the paid promotional opportunities Twitter has built into the platform.

Using Twitter Ads is an easy way to get your tweets in front of the audiences that don't yet follow you, which is particularly useful for generating new leads for your business. And you don't necessarily have to spend a fortune on it, either -- Twitter ads can be effective even on a relatively small budget.

How to Advertise on Twitter-Choose between "Promote Mode" and "Twitter Ads."

The first decision you need to make when setting up your Twitter ads is whether you'd like to promote individual tweets or run an entire ad campaign for a specific purpose.

Promoted Tweets vs. Twitter Ads

Promoted tweets will allow your tweets to appear in the Twitter streams or Twitter search results of specific users. Running Twitter Ads is a more holistic campaign, using multiple groups of tweets to accomplish a single goal for your brand. Depending on your objective, Twitter Ads can display your username in places other than a user's newsfeed, such as the "Who to Follow" section to the right of their Twitter homepage.

How do I choose?

If you're simply looking to get more eyeballs on a webpage, promoted tweets might be just the thing you need. In this option, you pay a flat monthly fee for as long as you're promoting a tweet. It's perfect for gaining focused exposure on (and generating leads from) a particular aspect of your business.

If you're looking to grow your follower base and/or build up your audience, Twitter Ads offer a bit more firepower.

.

Select your Twitter Ad's objective.

To launch a Twitter Ad campaign, your next step is determining your objective. You have a number of objectives to choose from, and you can see an elaboration of each objective once you select one on the Twitter Ads:

- App installs
- Followers
- Tweet engagements

- Promoted video views
- Website clicks or conversions
- App re-engagements
- In-stream video views (pre-roll)
- Awareness

Promoted Accounts

Ad campaigns focused on followers, the second objective listed above, are also known as "Promoted Accounts." This type of campaign allows you to promote your profile, rather than a series of tweets, in your target audience's newsfeeds and on the profile pages of the other accounts they care about.

Fill in the details of your ad campaign.

Once you choose an objective, you'll be taken to a page where you can name your campaign, a start and end date for your campaign, and your campaign's total budget. Depending on the objective you chose you might have other details to fill in that are unique to your ad. If your objective is app installs, for example, this step will require you to connect your app to Twitter, and then select this app from the dropdown shown below.

When determining how much money you want to invest in a Twitter Ads campaign, you'll set a daily budget and an optional total budget. Throughout the day, your daily budget will pay Twitter your set amount at the specific cadence you can set yourself.

The cadence of your promoted content can be set to "Standard (recommended)," which shows ads to your target audience at intervals Twitter deems most efficient; or "Accelerated," which shows your ads as much as possible throughout the day. Accelerated ads cater to ad campaigns you want to perform well in a short amount of time.

Create an ad group within your campaign.

Next, you'll create an ad group for your campaign -- there should be at least one pre-created on the left hand side of your Twitter Ads page. To create more than one ad group, select "Copy ad group" to the right hand side of your current ad group and you'll see new ones appear in your ad campaign's framework, as shown above.

Ad groups are individual ads that consist of their own budgets, audiences, and start and end times -- but operate under the umbrella of your larger campaign.

For example, if you have a two-week Twitter Ads campaign with the objective of website clicks and a budget of £75 you can also create one or more ad groups that run for just a couple of days each, promote separate webpages on your website, and target different types of Twitter users.

In the "Details" tab, enter an ad group name, a start and end time, a budget for the ad group, and a bid type. Bid types allow you to "bid" on a promoted ad placement. Ad placements will cost different amounts depending on your audience and where the ad appears on Twitter, and you can set your ad group to bid for placement in one of three ways:

- **Automatic bid:** This type of bid permits Twitter to bill you the most cost-effective amount every time your audience engages with your ad content. The cost Twitter bills you is based on your ad group's budget and audience parameters.

- **Maximum bid:** This type of bid gives you full control over how much money you're willing to pay every time your audience engages with your ad content.

- **Target bid:** This type of bid allows you to specify how much money from your ad group's budget you'd like Twitter to bill you every time your audience engages with your ad content. The price you're billed will reflect the *daily average cost* of each ad placement within your audience.

Select your target audience for each ad group.
Beneath the "Details" tab of your ad group, select "Targeting." This is where you'll set the parameters of your target audience. It's important to customize your audience to be a good fit for your company and your message. That way, you're only paying for engagement from people who might have some interest in downloading your content or learning more about your product or service. A more targeted audience is more likely to help you generate qualified leads.

What are my options?

To select an audience for each ad group you create, you'll customize the following criteria:

- **Gender:** If your product or service caters primarily to either males or females, you should take advantage of the gender targeting option.

- **Age:** Setting an age range is helpful for advertisements that are promoting a product or event that has either a particular age restriction or scope of interest.

- **Location:** You'll want to target by location if you run a local business, or if you sell primarily to specific regions

- **Language:** This criterion might need to be used in tandem with the location filter, described above, if an ad is targeting a region of the world that speaks a language other than English.

- **Device:** This is a great targeting option if your product or service caters more specifically to people on the go, or if your website visitors are most likely to convert on your offer when they're in the office.

- **Audience features:** These include keywords, movies & shows, conversation topics, events, and related interests.

115

You can also select which devices you'd like your promoted tweets to be displayed on -- any combination of desktop and the various mobile devices.

Targeting by Keywords

Targeting by "keywords"- an option included in the "Audience features" field, listed above -- allows you to reach people that search, tweet about, or engage with specific keywords. This audience targeting criterion is helpful if you want to know exactly how many Twitter users are currently using a keyword.

Targeting by Interests and Followers

Targeting by interests and followers allows you to create a list of Twitter usernames and then target users whose interests are similar to the interests of those users' followers. A great use of this type of targeting is when compiling a small list of the top influencers in your industry.

With this targeting option, you can also add a list of interest categories. So, for example, you could say, "show these tweets to people interested in marketing, social media, or lead generation." Again, this creates a broad audience focused on the topic of the content or products you're promoting.

Select the creatives you'd like to run with each ad group.

Your last task in creating a Twitter Ads campaign is to choose the creatives you want to run with each ad group belonging to your campaign. "Creatives" are simply the tweets you want to promote, and you can select them from the list of tweets that appear under each ad group's Creatives tab. Select the "Creatives" tab beneath the Targeting tab to get started. You can either select from existing tweets in your account or create new ones. To compose a new tweet, click the blue quill icon to the far right of your Creatives screen. When crafting a new tweet, you can check the "Promoted-only" button if you'd only like to promote it through your Twitter Ads campaign, and not have the tweet appear organically on your followers' newsfeeds.

In addition to promoting your tweets on your audiences' timelines, you can also choose to have your tweets appear in users' profiles and the detail pages of specific twitter conversations. The benefit of this type of targeting is that it helps you define a more qualified audience, since these people are actively looking for or engaging with those specific keywords that are relevant to your offer. You can select this option on the right hand side of your Creatives tab.

Review and launch your campaign.

Finally, select the "Review your campaign" button, to look over your campaign details. If everything looks correct, hit "Launch campaign" at the top-right hand corner of your screen to run the campaign.

How to Promote a Tweet

Promoting tweets allows you to show critical pieces of content to a wide audience and drive views to the landing pages that generate leads for your business. This Twitter Ads option gives you a lot more flexibility in terms of the content you want potential viewers and customers to see. Promoted tweets are paid advertisements that Twitter places in front of your target audience based on their interests or location. Each ad supports a single tweet, and you can customize the audience of each individual ad. Currently, businesses can only promote tweets in the U.S., U.K., and Japan.

1. Select "Promote Mode" from the campaign menu and click "Get started."

You'll start from the same place you start when creating a full, multi-tweet Twitter Ads campaign. Once there, click "Get started." When you're done, click "Next" on the top-righthand corner of the page.

2. Select your promoted tweet's country and timezone.

Start creating your ad by selecting of these three options, as well as your intended timezone. When you're done, click "Next" on the top-right hand corner of the page.

3. Choose either "Interests" or "Location" as your targeting method.

Twitter can promote tweets to an audience based on their interests or location. Choose one of these methods and follow Step 4 or Step 5, below, depending on your choice.

4. Choose up to five interests associated with your target audience.

If you choose to target an audience based on their interests, select this option, hit "Next," and Twitter will take you to the page shown above. Here, you can select a maximum of five interests related to your ideal audience. Keep in mind the more interests you select, the more types of people your promoted tweet will appear in front of.

5. Choose up to five locations associated with your target audience.

If you choose to target an audience based on their location, select this option, hit "Next," and Twitter will take you to the page shown above. Here, you can search a specific city, and country where you want your ad to appear. You can select up to five locations where you'd like your tweet to be promoted.

Review your ad criteria and select "Proceed."

Once you've customized your audience's interests or location, hit "Next" and Twitter will show you an overview of your ad criteria, including your bill.

Review your ad criteria and check that you agree to the Twitter Promote Mode's Terms of Service at the bottom of this page. Then, click "Proceed" on the top right-hand corner of your screen.

Measure and monitor your Twitter activity

As with the analytics function of other social media platforms, you can measure and monitor certain metrics in your Twitter account to analyse how well your posts are performing. This will help you find out the type of content that works best so you can make improvements.

Twitter metrics

Some important metrics include:

- **Number of followers:** See how many people follow your account over time. Analyse spikes and dips in new followers.

- **Impressions per tweet:** The number of people who saw your tweet in their timeline.

- **Engagements per tweet:** The number of times your tweet was interacted with. This includes, but is not limited to, people clicking images and links, re-tweeting and replying.

- **Link clicks per tweet:** The number of clicks on a link that has been included in your tweet. This is a particularly important engagement if your goals include driving traffic to your website.

- **Engagement rate:** The impressions received divided by your engagements gives a good indicator of how interesting or useful your audience finds your tweets.

- **Referrals:** Check your website analytics to see how important Twitter is in driving traffic to your site.

- **Conversions:** By adding a tracking code to links your tweet, you should be able to track how many conversions (eg sales or newsletter registrations) they generate.

You can also analyse your audience and see their demographics and interests. This offers a useful insight into who is following you and how to capture their attention.

Measurement tools

Twitter offers its own free analysis tool - **Twitter analytics** - which allows you to examine data about your tweets and audience. This information can also be downloaded into a spreadsheet for further analysis. If you use paid advertising, you will be able to see how this affects your impressions and engagements in comparison to organic posts. There are also other tools available from third parties that can help you analyse your Twitter activity.

Using website analytics such **Google Analytics** can also help you keep track of Twitter referrals and conversions. Tools such as Tweetdeck and Hootsuite can help you manage and keep track of your timeline and interactions. You can also save searches to help you follow online conversations and be aware of market trends.

Now read a summary of the main points from Chapter 6 overleaf.

****

In Summary

Using twitter for Social Media Marketing

- Twitter is one of the world's most popular social media platforms with over 335 million users (at 2021 but changes upwards all the time). Many businesses use Twitter to reach and connect with their customers. As with all social media networks, You need to consider if a twitter account will benefit your business. Are your competitors using it? How do other people in your industry use it? What success are your peers having on Twitter?

- Advantages of using Twitter as part of your social media marketing campaign: you can reach a wide audience; deliver customer service create brand identity and get Feedback. Cost is another major factor: It is free of charge to set up a Twitter account.

- Challenges of Twitter for business. It's important be aware of the downsides of Twitter for businesses. Resources: Maintaining a presence on Twitter requires a time commitment. It's also important that the staff looking after the account have the right skills and training. Criticism: Customers could complain publicly about product or services. Negative comments can reflect badly on your business. However dealing with complaints well can have a positive impact on your reputation.

Chapter 7

INSTAGRAM

Instagram as A Social Media Marketing Tool

> **Instagram**
>
> *Since its launch in 2010, Instagram (owned by facebook) has grown significantly. Below are some key facts that you should consider before deciding to add instagram to your arsenal of social media marketing platforms. You should ask yourself the usual questions: of what use is Instagram to my business; is it worth the time and effort and what will I gain from it? Hopefully, this chapter will enable you to see more clearly.*

Instagram originally launched as an iPhone-only application. Then came Android, then Web-profiles. Now, Instagram has become a social network that is more than just mobile — thanks to the Instagram feed now hitting the Web. Users can now log-in to see all of their friends photographic activity in the Instagram feed.

Facts:

- Instagram sees over one billion active monthly users and 500 million daily Instagram Stories.
- There are approximately 27.5 million users in the UK as at 2021.
- Instagram is the second most accessed network behind Facebook. Users browse for an average of 53 minutes per day.
- There are at least 25 million business profiles on Instagram.
- 90% of Instagram users follow at least one business, and 83% of users say Instagram has helped them discover new products and services.

It's very important to note that Instagram is intended for in-the-moment content. To stay relevant among your audience, you'll need to invest the resources required to post regularly. So, this is an important point for consideration-are you in a position to add Instagram to your strategy?

The best way to keep your followers engaged is to keep your Instagram profile up-to-date. If you don't have it already, download the Instagram app from the App Store or Google Play Store. You can view content on Instagram's website, but you can't upload it via your desktop. You'll need the app for that.

Setting up your instagram account

When you open the Instagram app, you'll have two choices for creating your account — *Log In With Facebook* or *Sign Up With*

Phone or Email. Be sure to sign up with a business email so your Instagram profile isn't linked to your personal Facebook account.

Next, enter your account details. Under *Full Name,* enter your actual business name so your profile is recognizable to visitors. This name is what's displayed on your profile; it isn't your account username (or handle). The *Username* is a name unique to your profile and allows other accounts to engage with your brand. Pick a username that is recognizable and easy to find. If your business name is taken, try to keep the first part of your business name in your username. *Note*: You can update your username later in your account settings, so don't worry if you want to change it in the future.

Optimising Your Instagram account

Now it's time to choose the right profile picture. Your profile picture is your first impression on new visitors. For this reason, keep your image consistent with your branding and visual markers. Consider using your logo or another familiar image. Instagram profile pictures are automatically cropped into a circle, so leave room around the corners of your image.

Create your Instagram bio.

Instagram bios have a 150-character maximum, so your goal here is a direct, concise summary of who you are and why people should follow you. Tell your audience about your business using a hint of personality. Instagram bios aren't searchable, so don't worry about keywords or hashtags.

In your bio, you can encourage users to take a specific action, such as using a certain hashtag or visiting your website. Your bio is the only place where you can feature a clickable URL and drive traffic to an external site. For future edits, click on the *Edit Profile* button on your profile to change your photo, name, username, bio, and URL.

Managing Your Instagram settings

Lastly, review your account settings. Click on the three stacked lines in the upper right-hand corner of your profile, then click on *Settings* at the bottom of the window. Within your settings, you'll be able to do things like change your password, see posts you've liked, enable notifications, and much more. Here are a few things you should check out right away.

Story Settings, where you can manage who can see and reply to your Instagram Stories. We recommend allowing all your followers to see and reply to your Stories to increase brand engagement. From your settings, click *Privacy > Story* to access your Story Controls. (You can also access this by clicking the gear icon in the top left corner when posting a story.)

Switch to a Professional Account, which allows you to identify your profile as a business profile. Instagram's Business Tools feature makes it easy for users to contact you, provides you with in-depth insights, and allows you to promote your content. Your business must have a Facebook business page to switch to an

Instagram business profile. From your settings, click *Account >
Switch to Professional Account* to access these features.

To switch to a business profile, choose this setting, log into
Facebook, and allow Instagram to manage your Pages. Select a
Facebook Page to connect to your Instagram profile.

Instagram will automatically import relevant information
from your Facebook page for you to edit. You now have an
Instagram business profile. Be sure to check out your profile
insights and account settings!

Private Account, where you can change your profile from public
to private. Instagram will automatically set your profile to public.
As a business, you'll want users to see your posts and follow
your business without any obstacles. From your settings, click
Privacy > Account Privacy, and make sure that's turned off.

Comments, which allows you to hide comments with certain
keywords or phrases. To do this, you must enter the specific
words and phrases into your Instagram settings and turn on the
feature. Receiving comments is exciting and encouraging, but
certain comments may go against brand values or offend your
audience. From your settings, click *Privacy > Comments* to
update these.

Adding Additional Instagram Accounts, where you can add up
to five accounts and switch between them without logging in
and out. This feature also allows you to have multiple people

logged into an account at one time. To add an account, click *Add Account* at the bottom of your settings. Enter the username and password of the account you'd like to add. To switch between accounts, go to your profile and tap your username at the top of the screen. Choose the account you'd like to switch to.

Types of Instagram posts

Now that you've created and optimized your Instagram account, it's time to start posting content. Instagram allows you to post several types of content, including photos, videos, and Stories.

Images-The most common post on Instagram is an image post. When posting images, share a variety of photos. Variety will show your brand is diverse and engage your followers in different ways. It's also important to remember that Instagram users are looking for genuine posts from brands — not blatant advertisements. Try to capture your company culture with lifestyle shots and behind-the-scenes looks. Avoid posting too many photos of your product. As you start to explore the platform, you'll see there are countless kinds of images you can post to your account. Take note of any concepts or styles you think would work well for your brand.

Behind the scenes posts-These posts offer a glimpse into the part of your business that people don't normally see. It's important that they don't look staged. Make them as authentic as possible.

Educational Posts-Educational posts offer tips on how to do or make something. The photos or videos usually present the instructions in a way that are quick and easy to follow.

Influencer Posts-As we have seen, Influencer posts use the fame of a celebrity or well-known public figure to promote your brand. These posts often include a visual of the influencer using or interacting with your product. One of the main benefits of influencer posts is gaining the attention of another audience.

Motivational Posts-A motivational post combines a simple visual with an overlaid quote or uplifting text. These posts encourage your audience and amplify your brand values. While effective, try to post these sparingly to avoid looking cheesy. Apps like Quipio and Typic can help you add text to photos in a way that's consistent with your brand guidelines.

User-Generated Content

Similar to employee reposts, user-generated content (UGC) is curated content from your fans and followers. Your tagged posts and posts with your brand hashtag are a great source for UGC. Sharing your fans' and followers' photos not only make the original poster feel good, it also shows that you truly care about your customers. Just be sure to credit the original post with a tag or in the caption. To repost user-generated content, screenshot and crop the original post or use a reposting app like Repost for Instagram.

Capturing and Editing Instagram Photos

Now that we've explored what you can post on Instagram, let's review some ways to make sure your content is successful. Unlike other social media platforms, Instagram's simple profile layout forces you to focus on the quality of content ... not the quantity. While this is great for engagement, it also means that you can't hide mediocre content. Do your very best to use high-resolution images on your Instagram feed.

Square images should be 1080 x 1080px. Landscape images should be 1080 x 566px, and profile images should be 1350 x 1080px. Regardless of what size you upload, every image will be shown as a square in your profile feed.

Taking a Photo With Your Smartphone

As we have seen with YouTube videos, quality photography is no longer limited to those with professional cameras. You can take eye-catching photos using a tool you already have in your hands, Your phone.

How to Add Filters and Edit Photos

Thanks to Instagram's built-in tools and filters, editing photos is very simple. First, start with a good quality photo. No amount of editing can fix photos if they have poor composition or lighting. Consider using other apps to edit your photo. Snapseed is a free editing app that allows you to apply effects like HDR and tonal contrast as well as adjust brightness, contrast, and saturation.

VSCO is also another popular editing app with numerous free filters that resemble popular film stocks.

When you upload your edited photo to Instagram, it'll automatically crop your photo into a square. To change it back to the original width, press the icon (the two outward facing arrows). At this stage, you can add additional Instagram filters. Each Instagram filter has its own personality that can drastically change a photo. Next, try adjusting your photo lux. According to Instagram, "Lux balances the exposure and provides much needed brightness" to photos. Lux make can make your image more vibrant and bring out details. To do this, press the wand icon at the top of the screen and adjust the level.

Videos

Instagram also lets you upload videos — as long as they're a minute or less in length. You can download professionally edited videos from your computer or videos you've edited in a mobile app. They can be the videos you have put together for YouTube. Splice is a free editing tool that allows you to cut together multiple clips and add transitions, titles, and music. Instagram videos default to playing *without* sound. Because of this, make sure at least the first few seconds of your videos don't need sound to be understood. You can use your caption or prompt viewers to turn on the sound.

Boomerangs-Open your Instagram and tap the camera icon in the top left-hand corner of the home screen. This is the in-app camera. You can also access this by swiping right on the screen.

Notice the settings on the bottom. The *Normal* setting, to which the camera defaults, takes still photos. You'll see that the first setting to the right is *Boomerang*, which takes three-second, looping videos that play forwards and backwards.

Instagram Stories

Instagram Stories allow users to post at a higher frequency without overposting and clogging up your main feed. Stories usually feature less-polished, more organic images and videos. Like Snapchat Stories, your Instagram Story disappears after 24 hours.

Stories are all about authenticity. While your Instagram feed should feature polished photos, Stories can be a little more raw. Use the feature to give a behind-the-scenes look at your brand or showcase your company culture. Stories are also a helpful tool to showcase live events your business hosts or attends, as this feature is much more time-sensitive.

How to Post to Your Instagram Story

Instagram offers three options for posting to your Story. You can tap the camera in the upper left corner, tap *Your Story* above your feed, or just swipe right to access the camera.

Like your typical phone camera, the thunderbolt Icon controls the flash and the arrow icon switches the camera view between front and forward-facing. Instagram has recently added filters (like on Snapchat) that you can access by tapping the smiling face next to the arrow icon.

Stories make it easy to add personality to your content! Swipe to the left or right to access the filters. Select the pen icon to choose a colour and add a doodle. Press the *Aa* icon add text with your keyboard. The smile icon allows you to add a location, GIF, music, poll, and many more fun features. Instagram also allows you to tag another account in your Story, which is a great way to connect with other businesses and your followers. To tag someone, type the "@" followed by the username you'd like to mention. This makes the tag clickable so that viewers can visit the tagging profile. You'll receive a notification if you've been mentioned in someone's story.

When you're ready to publish, press the *Your Story* icon or save it to your camera roll to publish later. You can also tap *Send To* to add to your Story as well as send directly to other users. Stories appear at the top of the Instagram feed and through your profile picture. To see who viewed your content, swipe up when viewing your Story.

Instagram Story Highlights

Instagram Story Highlights are Instagram Stories that have been preserved past their 24-hour limit and posted to an Instagram profile. You can find them in the small circles under an Instagram bio. Story Highlights are a fantastic way to showcase your best stories and post them semi-permanently to your account for your followers to see. They're also useful ways to showcase products, services, promotions, and more as your Highlights can include links to external sites.

0

There are multiple ways to add Instagram Story Highlights. It's important to note, however, that you can't add images or video directly to your Story Highlights. Your Story Highlights need to be a previously-posted (or currently live) Instagram Story before you can pin it to a Highlight (or create a new Highlight).

One way to create and/or post to a Story Highlight is with a current Instagram Story. Open your current Instagram Story and click the heart icon labeled *Highlight*. At this point, Instagram will ask you which Highlight you'd like to pin the Story to, or it will ask you to create a Highlight if you don't have any yet.

As we discussed above, Instagram has a live video option that allows you to share content real time. To start a live video stream, open the Instagram camera, swipe to the *Live* setting, and click the button to *Start Live Video*.

Find Your Instagram Voice

Every social platform has a distinct voice. What works on Twitter may not work on Instagram. On Instagram, posts with a lighthearted, authentic tone tend to perform the best.

Experiment with emojis and other fun tools to give your brand a distinct feel. Don't expect to get it right the first time — it can take a while to develop your brand's voice. If you're ever in doubt about what to write, keep it short. There's little correlation between caption length and engagement, but short captions allow your visuals do the talking.

Hashtags

Hashtags refer to keywords or keyword phrases that are spelled without spaces and prefaced with a pound (#) sign. They are generally used to reference events, conferences, pop culture, entertainment, or recurring themes and are a great way to make your content more visible. Originally popularized by Twitter, hashtags are now on multiple social networks.

Using Hashtags on Instagram

Instagram feeds are always changing, which makes sense considering that 80 million photos are shared everyday. With that much content, it can be difficult for your account to get noticed. That's where hashtags come in handy.

On Instagram, hashtags aggregate posts from a wide variety of users into a single feed … although only public accounts can be shown when searching hashtags. Instagram makes it simple and easy for users to find tagged content. When you search a word or phrase, the search results page shows you four parts:

1. **Top**, which displays the top Instagram accounts, hashtags, and locations that include your keyword (typically accounts that are popular or that you're following)
2. **Accounts**, which shows you the top Instagram accounts that include your keyword

3. **Tag**s, which suggests popular hashtags that include your keyword and how many other Instagram posts have been shared with that hashtag
4. **Places**, which displays nearby locations that include your keyword.

For example, if you're planning on tagging your post with #books, you may want to tag related tags like #bookshops, #bookworm, or #goodreads to broaden your post reach. Using hashtags is easy enough. Simply create hashtags using characters, numbers, or emojis; you can add up to thirty to the caption. Just remember — your account *must* be public for your posts to appear on hashtag feeds.

Many businesses use their own hashtags to roll out a new product, manage an Instagram campaign, promote an event, and collect user-generated content. If you'd like to do this for your business, make sure yours isn't being used for another purpose ... and then encourage your audience to use it!

Instagram marketing strategy
Since Instagram is *very* different from other popular social sites, it requires a distinct marketing strategy. You need to develop your brand's own unique style.
1. Set your goals for Instagram.
Before you start posting on Instagram, ask yourself (or your team) one thing: Why are you on Instagram? As popular as the platform is, your answer shouldn't be, "*... because everyone else*

is." To be successful on Instagram in the long-run, you must have a set purpose and goals so you can justify your time, energy, and monetary investment.

2. Determine your Instagram audience.

The same message for all of the social media sites. Determine the audience you want to reach *before* you begin marketing on Instagram. If you have other marketing strategies in place, draw from those to keep your efforts consistent. Don't forget to consider factors like age, location, gender, income, interests, motivations, and pain points.

3. Conduct a competitive analysis.

After you determine your Instagram audience, do a competitive analysis to see what other marketers in your field are posting. If you already know your top competitors, start by reviewing their Instagram profiles. If not, search for terms related to your business and industry to find similar accounts. Conduct a quick audit of related accounts to see what posts are getting the highest engagement, what popular hashtags they're using, what their captions are, how often they post, and how quickly they're growing. This information can serve as a benchmark as you start growing your own account.

While auditing your competitors' content, take note of any opportunities they might've missed. Adding unique content into the mix will help your business to stand out from the rest.

4. Configure an editorial calendar.

On average, brands post about six images per week on Instagram ... which is over 300 posts per year! At that frequency, it can be difficult to keep track what you need to post *and* what's already posted. Creating an editorial calendar can help you save time and manage your Instagram presence. Fill in your calendar with some Instagram post types discussed earlier and plan your captions, hashtags, and posting times in advance.

Your editorial calendar is also a great place to record any key events to highlight on your Instagram account, such as new product launches or special offers. With an editorial calendar, you can keep an eye out for real-time opportunities instead of scrambling for last-minute posts.

5. Build a consistent brand on Instagram.

Random or disjointed content confuses your audience and can cause you to lose followers. To prevent this, maintain a consistent brand aesthetic on your Instagram account. Determine what this looks like by thinking about your brand personality. What are your brand values? How would your customers and employees define your brand? Are you bold, playful, gritty, or adventurous? Once you determine your brand personality, refine your content to match. This can even apply to the colour palette used in your photos.

Grow your Instagram follower base.

Growing your following takes serious time and energy. You may be tempted to take the easy way out and buy followers … don't do this! Purchasing followers won't actually drive engagement, which is really what you need to ensure your posts are being seen. (Also, Instagram's recent API changes will automatically delete those followers!)

Make sure your username is recognizable and searchable. If people can't find you, they can't follow you! Fill out your bio. It's the last thing someone sees before they make the decision to follow you so be sure to include who you are and what you do.

Once your profile is optimized start posting. It's a good idea to populate your feed with ten to 15 high-quality posts before you really start engaging people. If users visit your profile and find it empty, they probably won't follow you. Then, start following accounts that interest you and relate to your business. Think of Instagram like a community and look for other businesses in your area or influencers who might enjoy your product or service. As you follow accounts, Instagram will suggest related ones that you can follow, too.

After you follow an account, interact with their content. This is the most natural way to draw attention to your own Instagram account without being spammy. When you follow or interact with an account, the account owner will get a notification. This could prompt them to check out your account and start following you. Always appreciate your followers by responding to their comments and engaging with their content.

Encourage others to share your content. Invite brand ambassadors to share your account or collaborate with similar accounts.

Lastly, be sure to promote your Instagram on other channels. Include an Instagram social share button on your website and share your Instagram on other social platforms. Sometimes the fastest way to gain more followers is to simply ask for them!

7. Convert your Instagram followers into customers.

Once you establish a dedicated follower base, you can start converting those followers into paying customers. Below are some strategies.

- Promotions: Deals, discounts, BOGOFs, and other offerings are a great way to drive first-time sales with your Instagram audience. Be sure to include what your followers need to do to receive the offer, and mention a deadline to create a sense of urgency.
- Contests: What better way to make someone a customer than by letting them try your product? Run contests that require someone to follow your account or post with a hashtag to enter.
- Teasers: Instagram is a great platform to show your audience glimpses of new products before they're available. While you don't want to spam your followers' feeds with only product photos, a few images can build excitement.
- Live launches: Consider showcasing a new product or service using Instagram Live. Then, drive users to purchase by including a purchase link in your bio.

- Also, don't forget to leverage the link in your Instagram bio as well as your Instagram Story Highlights as these can connect followers to your website, blog, and product pages.

Now read a summary of the main points from Chapter 7 overleaf.

****

In Summary

Using Instagram as a tool for social media marketing

- There are at least 25 million business profiles on Instagram. 90% of Instagram users follow at least one business, and 83% of users say Instagram has helped them discover new products and services.

- It's very important to note that Instagram is intended for in-the-moment content. To stay relevant among your audience, you'll need to invest the resources required to post regularly. So, this is an important point for consideration-are you in a position to add Instagram to your strategy? The best way to keep your followers engaged is to keep your Instagram profile up-to-date.

- Instagram allows you to post several types of content, including photos, videos, and Stories.

- Every social platform has a distinct voice. What works on Twitter may not work on Instagram. On Instagram, posts with a light hearted, authentic tone tend to perform the best. Experiment with emojis and other fun tools to give your brand a distinct feel.

- Since Instagram is *very* different from other popular social sites, it requires a distinct marketing strategy. You need to develop your brand's own unique style.

****

Chapter 8

PINTEREST

Pinterest as A Social Media Marketing Tool

What is Pinterest?

Pinterest is a visual discovery engine for finding ideas like recipes, home and style inspiration, and more. It is a different concept to the other social media sites that we have seen so far.

Think of Pinterest as a virtual pinboard or bulletin board, but with organizational and tools. If you're interested in a subject, such as cooking or decorating, find images you like on Pinterest or on the web, and then save those images to your Pinterest bulletin board. Create multiple bulletin boards to catalog your interests. For example, create a wedding board, a recipe board, and a decorating board.

Pinterest is also a social network. Users interact by following each other and by liking and commenting on images, similar to Facebook or Instagram. Save someone else's images to your boards, and private message people with whom you share interests.

Home feed

Your home feed is where you'll find Pins, people, and brands based on your recent activity. You can also see Pins from the people, topics, and boards you choose to follow. You can also search for Pins by typing in keywords into the search bar.

Pins

Pins are bookmarks that people use to save ideas they love on Pinterest. If you click through the Pin, you can visit the website to learn how to make it or where to buy it. As you discover Pins you like, click the red Save button to save them to your boards.

When you try a Pin, you can show people on Pinterest how it went. Sometimes you'll find a Pin that you know a friend will like. Send Pins directly to a friend or a group in a message to pass the inspiration around. You can also use Messages to chat with your friends, whether or not you shared a Pin. You can see your messages by clicking on your computer or tapping followed by **Inbox** on your mobile device.

Boards

The Pins you save live on your boards. Name your boards and arrange them on your profile however you want. Invite other people on Pinterest to collaborate on Group boards to find even more ideas. To organize your Pins within boards, create board sections. Add a "Tents" or "Camping" hacks section to your Camping board to keep similar ideas in the same place. There are no rules - organize your Pins in whatever way makes sense to you!

If you prefer to keep your Pins private you can make your board secret. Only you and anyone you invite can see your secret boards.

Profile

Find all the Pins you save, boards you create, and Pins you try in your profile. You can also see who's following you and the boards, topics, and people you follow. Anyone can see your profile, but your secret boards will stay hidden. You can see your secret boards when you view your own profile. Your profile is not just a collection of the ideas you like - it's a reflection of who you are. It's where all your ideas and inspiration for projects past, present, and future live.

How to Get Started Using Pinterest

To get up and running with Pinterest, create a free Pinterest account:

1. Go to Pinterest.com. You'll see a slideshow that gives you an idea of the types of subjects Pinterest can inspire.
2. Select **About**, **Business**, or **Blog** from the upper-right corner of the page to learn more about Pinterest.
3. Select **Sign up** in the upper-right corner of the web page.
4. Enter your email, create a password, enter your age, and select **Continue.**
5. Or, sign up using your Facebook or Google account.
6. You'll see a **Welcome to Pinterest** message. Select **Next** to continue.

7. Choose a gender identity.

8. Select a language, then choose your country or region.

9. Select some areas of interest (you can add more later),

10. Then select **Done**.

Pinterest builds an initial home feed based on your interests.

- Click a Pin you would like to learn more about it. You'll see who uploaded the image and any comments.
- Select **Save** to save the image to a board.
- Select the **arrow** next to the number of comments to add a comment.
- Select **Follow** to follow the uploader and see their Pins.

When you select **Save**, you're prompted to create a new board. Name the board and select **Create**. The next time you select and save an image, Pinterest gives you the option of saving it to your current board or creating a new board.

At any time, select **Home** to go back to your home feed. The Pins you see are continually updated based on the Pins you've liked and saved.

Go to the **Today** tab in the upper-left corner to see trending ideas and topics relevant to your interests.

Go to the **Following** tab to see the latest pins from people and boards you follow, and to find suggestions on who to follow based on your interests.

How to Save a Pin From the Web

You're not limited to saving pins that are on Pinterest. If you're browsing the web and come across something perfect for your board, you can add it as below:

1. From your Pinterest home page, select the **plus sign** in the lower-right corner of the page.
2. Select **Get our browser button** or **Create a Pin**.
3. To use the browser button, you need to use Chrome, Firefox, or Edge.
4. If you selected **Get our browser button**, select **Got it** from the next screen.
5. You'll see a **plus sign** on the browser toolbar. Select it and then select **Install** to install the browser extension.
6. Open the website with an image you want to Pin, hover the cursor over the image, and select **Pinterest Save** (the Pinterest logo with the word **Save** next to it).
7. Choose a board and select **Save**.

If you don't want to install a browser button extension, select the **plus sign** and then select **Create a Pin**.

1. Select **Save from site**.
2. Enter the website URL and select the arrow to continue.
3. Select an image and then choose **Add to Pin**.
4. Add a title, select a board from the drop-down menu, then select **Save**.

Follow individual boards

Sometimes, you may not want to follow an account, but you like one of its boards. If you want to follow an individual board to see when new Pins are added to it:

1. Select the Pin that interests you.
2. Toward the bottom of the box, select the **board title**. In this example, it's **Whole30**.
3. You're taken to the board's page. Select **Follow** to see new Pins added to this board.

Navigating account options

Select the **drop-down arrow** from the upper-right menu to see more options. You'll go through each of these options in the next several steps to see where each takes you.

- **Add another account** takes you to a screen where you can create a new Pinterest account and switch between accounts.
- **Add a free business account** helps you set up a business account, so you can run ads, access analytics, and more.
- **Settings** brings you to a screen where you can edit your account profile, add a photo, change account settings, choose notification settings, see and change privacy settings, turn on two-factor authentication, and more.
- **Tune your home feed** brings you to a screen where you can edit your preferences and interests.

- **Install the [browser] app** allows you to install an app that lets a Pinterest tab run in the background when you're using a Pinterest-optimized browser.
- **Get Help** brings up the Pinterest Help Center.
- **See terms and privacy** brings up the Pinterest privacy policy.
- Selecting **Log out** will log you out of Pinterest.

Account Info

To see your followers, who you're following, and more:

1. Select your **account** icon or profile picture, if you set one.
   When **Boards** is selected, you'll see your current boards.

The above is a brief description of Pinterest. It might not be your first choice when deciding to put forward a social media strategy but it is good to know what you can achieve with the site if you do decide to set up an account.

Now read a summary of the main points from chapter 8 overleaf.

****

In Summary

Using Pinterest as a tool for social media marketing

■ Pinterest is a visual discovery engine for finding ideas like recipes, home and style inspiration, and more. It is a slightly different concept to the other social media sites that we have seen so far. Pinterest is also a social network. Users interact by following each other and by liking and commenting on images, similar to Facebook or Instagram.

■ Think of Pinterest as a virtual pinboard or bulletin board, but with organizational and bookmarking tools. If you're interested in a subject, such as cooking or decorating, find images you like on Pinterest or on the web, and then save those images to your Pinterest bulletin board. Create multiple bulletin boards to catalog your interests. For example, create a wedding board, a recipe board, and a decorating board.

■ Pins are bookmarks that people use to save ideas they love on Pinterest. If you click through the Pin, you can visit the website to learn how to make it or where to buy it. As you discover Pins you like, click the red Save button to save them to your boards.

■ When you try a Pin, you can show people on Pinterest how it went. Sometimes you'll find a Pin that you know a friend will like. Send Pins directly to a friend or a group in a message to pass the inspiration around. You can also use Messages to chat with your friends, whether or not you shared a Pin. You can see your messages by clicking on your computer or tapping followed by Inbox on your mobile device.

■ Boards. The Pins you save live on your boards. Name your boards and arrange them on your profile however you want. Invite other people on Pinterest to collaborate on Group boards to find even more ideas.

■ Profile. Find all the Pins you save, boards you create, and Pins you try in your profile. You can also see who's following you and the boards, topics, and people you follow. Anyone can see your profile, but your secret boards will stay hidden. You can see your secret boards when you view your own profile. Your profile is not just a collection of the ideas you like - it's a reflection of who you are. It's where all your ideas and inspiration for projects past, present, and future live.

****

Conclusion

This book has been wide ranging and the emphasis throughout has been on how to set up the various platforms and how you can use them to enhance your business. There have been many who, over the years, have waxed lyrical in terms of the wonders of social media and its positive effect on your business. However, for certain, the proof of the pudding is in the eating and the first thing to do is to actually set up the various sites and in the process develop your own skills in social media marketing. Skills development and raised awareness will happen as you go.

I have tried to emphasise that social media marketing should sit alongside other more traditional forms of marketing that you might do. Certainly, using social media sites such as Facebook and Twitter, plus the other sites covered, is far less expensive in terms of financial outlay than the more traditional forms such as newspapers, TV etc. However, where setting up and utilising social media sites is more expensive is in terms of the time expended in maintenance and development of the sites.

The maintenance of the sites mentioned in this book is the big investment in time and, it is hoped that your business can reap the rewards. I would recommend taking a step-by-step approach to setting up sites, probably starting with Facebook, until you feel confident then develop your strategy. You can also look closely at the benefits of each site and decide which ones would most benefit your business. For example, would time spent setting up and maintaining an Instagram page really benefit your business?

Finally, we are in a changing business environment. The switch to online shopping, and the increased use of social media, has markedly increased. Deciding to use social media platforms can only be a positive step forward.

Good luck with your venture!

Useful websites

The below sites are a small selection of the main sites connected with each area. There are many more dealing with all the main sites.

Facebook

www.facebook.com/business/pages/set-up

hootsuite.com/steps-to-create-a-facebook-business-page

bizfluent.com/how-7555382-create-business-facebook-account

www.thebalancesmb.com/how-to-customize-a-business-page-on facebook

YouTube

youtubemarketingtools.com

smallbusinessbc.ca/article/how-use-youtube-effective-marketing

shanebarker.com/blog/youtube-marketing-tools

www.techsmith.com (Video production site)

LinkedIn

www.linkedin.com/help

business.linkedin.com/en-uk/marketing-solutions/blog/posts

https://business.linkedin.com/business page (setting up a business page) www.businessknowhow.com/internet/create-linkedin-business-page

Twitter
help.twitter.com/en/using-twitter/create-twitter-account

business.twitter.com/en/basics/create-a-twitter-business-profile
(Creating a business page on Twitter)

www.lifewire.com/join-twitter-by-setting-up-account

Instagram
business.instagram.com/shopping/setup

blogs.constantcontact.com/getting-started-instagram

Pinterest
business.pinterest.com (Setting up a Pinterest Business Account)

meanttobemade.com/pinterest-set-up

www.lifewire.com/get-a-pinterest-account-

Online marketing
www.shopify.co.uk

www.shopwired.co.uk

blog.hubspot.com/marketing/social-media-marketing

****